WONDER, FEAR, AND LONGING

A BOOK OF PRAYER

MARK YACONELLI

ZONDERVAN®

ZONDERVAN.com/
AUTHORTRACKER
follow your favorite authors

CONTENTS

All prayer rises from the heart of our experience. We are human beings, and human beings are a creative concoction of emotions, attitudes, memories, fantasies, desires, physical aches, and thoughtful reflection. Hurting, we cry, "Mercy." Awed, we whisper, "Thank you." Yearning, we plead, "Show me the way." The prayers of the Bible—the psalms, the prophets, the prayers of David and Sarah and Mary and Paul and so many others—are a messy human mixture of humbling gratitude, trembling awe, heartfelt compassion, desperate need, violent hatred, erotic desire, and dreamy hope. Just like the people in the Scriptures, we too are invited to offer God all that lives within our tangled hearts and minds. Every time we pray we're invited to expose the truth of who we are. Prayer makes us more real— and it is through prayer that we learn the shocking truth: It is our real selves (not our "spiritual selves") whom God loves and desires most deeply.

It is one of the tragedies of religion that prayer has been made into a chore, a discipline, an obligation—something devout people are supposed to do. Great harm has been done to many of us trained to believe prayer is a thing that needs study and practice, a discipline with stages and levels, special words and formulas. But right and wrong, correct and incorrect, are not categories for prayer. Too many churches and pastors give the impression that real prayer requires special training. These misguided teachings make prayer feel formal and awkward, like reading a speech to someone you're madly in love with.

Prayer isn't a performance. Prayer isn't a ladder to God. There are no essential steps in prayer because there is nowhere to go in prayer. There is nothing you need to accomplish in prayer. Prayer is simply remembering you already have all you need. The surprise of prayer—and this surprise never gets old—is that God is already waiting, listening, and cradling the deepest depths of who you are. Prayer is recalling that God really is that loving companion who is closer to you than your own breathing, nearer than your own heartbeat, already holding with compassion all the parts within you that you find too difficult to acknowledge. No prayer can ever bring God any closer. Already, without any effort on your part, God patiently dwells within the tender recesses of your own heart.

In prayer, we enter into the relationship we already have with God. In prayer, we give attention to the intimate, sacred communication that is ongoing within us. Prayer is not something we make up; it is something we discover, something we allow, something we yield to. "Only through prayer do we come to know our own goodness and the love that God has for us," Brother Rogers counsels. Through prayer we become aware, receptive, and responsive to God's love in the midst of all things, all people, and all experiences.

Imagine you are sitting next to someone who is deeply in love with you. Imagine this person gazes on you with wonder and delight. Imagine this person is safe, gentle, and comfortable to be with. Imagine you can trust this person with your whole self.

What is it you would say to such a person?

Would you speak your secret hopes and fantasies?

Would you expose your deepest hurt and shame?

Would you ask for help?

Would you listen, or talk, or just sit quietly enjoying the warmth of your loved one's gaze?

These are the kind of questions prayer invites.

This book invites you to pray ten aspects of your experience as a human being. Each chapter begins with some opening reflections and then offers four sections to help draw you into prayer. The first section, "Scripture," presents selected verses from the Bible that offer words and images intended to open you toward God. This is followed by "Prayer," where I've placed various written prayers that might help you find words that express your own heart to God. "Meditation" is the next section, offering various thoughts from other praying Christians that are meant to help you deepen your own reflection and understanding of God in prayer.

The final section, "Contemplation," offers a variety of exercises to help expand your own experience of prayer. Contemplation is a big word with a very simple meaning—the word actually means to "dwell in God's temple." Ultimately, the exercises in this final section are designed to help you dwell with God. Sometimes the exercises are creative, inviting you to write, draw, go outdoors, or use your imagination. Other exercises invite you to try a method of prayer that has ancient roots in the Christian tradition.

As you peruse the various Scriptures, prayers, meditations, and contemplative exercises, remember that the hope of this book is that you will be inspired to turn and pray. So as you read, notice when you feel drawn to prayer. It might be a particular story, a word in a verse, a meditative thought or an idea within an exercise that sends you toward prayer. Be sensitive to your own heart and willing to set the book aside whenever you find yourself drawn toward God.

A few other suggestions for using this book:

*   Find a hospitable place to read, a place where you feel safe and free to pray. Remember that Jesus liked to wander off into deserted regions when he needed to pray. Look for a place where you won't be distracted or interrupted, a place that's comfortable, a place where you might take a nap if you wanted to. If possible, find a place outside: A back yard, a creek side, the hill behind a housing development, an abandoned bench on the church grounds. If you can't go outside, find an indoor place where you won't be disturbed—your bedroom, a nook within a library, a chair by the fireplace, an empty church sanctuary. When you find a place to read and pray you might begin by lying down. Lie down—on the grass, on the

bench, on the carpeted floor of your bedroom—and open yourself before God. Hand over all the desires and disappointments you carry within you to God. Release whatever struggle, shame, or hardship lies within you. Put your hands over your heart, then lie down and surrender yourself to love...

* You might want to add some variety and creativity to this time of reading and praying. Bring crayons and paper, a journal, or other creative media with you when you pray. Let your time in prayer be playful. Feel free to draw, paint, journal, or dance. If you're outside, write your prayers in the dirt. Float your prayers down a creek. Make this book useful—scribble words in the margins, draw pictures on the inside cover, tear out a poem or verse you like and carry it in your pocket.

* Remember that prayer is a learning process. In prayer we're learning who we are; we're learning how to live our lives; we're learning how to trust our darkness and fear to God; we're learning how to give ourselves over to the same Divine Love that Jesus carried. Prayer is a school of spiritual living in which God serves as teacher. Remember that

God tutors each of us uniquely in the ways of prayer. Your way of praying will be different from the ways others pray, and it will change as you grow older. This is why it's helpful to journal your prayers. When you write your prayers, you can sometimes see the growth that's taking place.

* Sometimes it's helpful to talk to others about your prayers. Our experiences of prayer can sometimes be overpowering or confusing. Remember that Jesus expects his friends to rely on one another. If something happens in your prayer that is perplexing or confusing, scary or deeply moving, go and share this with a trusted Christian—a pastor, a family member, a person in your church, a good soul friend. Sometimes we understand our prayers best by talking them out with others.

Prayer is an act of trust. Each time you pray, trust that God is working to free you for greater life and love. Trust God, even when your prayer feels dull and flat. Every time you turn and pray, trust that in some hidden way your soul is being watered and tended.

Christians throughout history have discovered that it is in prayer that God teaches us to express our sufferings, claim our yearnings, and respond with gratitude to the frightening wonder of being alive. It is through prayer that God teaches us real rest, real freedom, real truth, real inspiration, and real compassion. It is in prayer that we are found, in prayer that we are welcomed, in prayer that God meets us, celebrates us, heals us, and awakens us to the life of Jesus.

So...

Whatever your age, whatever your situation, whether your life feels broken and full of despair or bursting with love and life, whether you are lying in a field of grass or reading in bed with a flashlight, know you have this moment

right now

and in this moment

there is God,

a loving God,

a compassionate God,

a God who waits quietly within your own heart,

a God who is "mercy, within mercy, within mercy."[1]

So what are you waiting for?

All is ready.

Here you are.

Let us pray.

---

[1] Thomas Merton, *The Sign of Jonas* (Houghton Mifflin Harcourt, 2002).

LOVE

CHAPTER ONE

God is love, and those who abide in love
abide in God, and God abides in them.

1 JOHN 4:16

Love God.
Love others as you love yourself.

Jesus once said the Christian faith was expressed in these two statements.

We spend much of our lives dealing with the second principle. We constantly struggle with our relationships with people—family, friends, teachers, coworkers, obnoxious strangers. We know what Jesus is talking about when he asks us to love others; he means we're to show kindness, patience, generosity, and truthfulness in our interactions with other people. He means we're to treat others as we want to be treated.

We also know what Jesus is referring to when he says, "As you love yourself." He wants us to try to see ourselves the way God sees us, the way a loving parent would see us. He means seeing ourselves as God's beloved. He means we should offer ourselves the same kindness, compassion, patience, encouragement, and truthfulness we seek to offer others.

Jesus encourages every human being to engage in this work (and it often feels like work) each day. To live with and value other people, to live with and value ourselves.

But Jesus says the first and most essential struggle in which a Christian engages is not this effort to love ourselves and others. The first struggle is to receive and return God's love, the love that rises from the very center of every living thing.

Have you ever felt truly loved? When you're really loved, whether it's by a parent or a friend or someone you're romantically attracted to, you feel a sense of well being all the way down to your bones. When you're loved well, there's a sense of freedom, a sense of safety, a feeling that you can really be yourself without fear of rejection or humiliation. Sometimes it's energizing to be loved—you feel inspired, encouraged, creative, less anxious, less irritable. You find yourself feeling more generous, compassionate, more likely to bring food to a homeless person. Every human being wants and needs love—anyone who tells you otherwise is lying.

God knows that every human heart needs love. At the same time God grieves that most of us are not loved very well. Human beings are broken and fearful, and sadly we often show the most cruelty, anger, and indifference to our family members, our good friends, and others who are closest to us. And yet beneath the broken love human beings exchange with one another, God comes to us. Beneath the hurt and longing, Christians experience and trust a deeper love that has been made visible and accessible in Jesus. Christians have known, and felt, and been changed by this God-love that comes to every person unearned, as a gift.

Christians trust that this love is more powerful, more healing, and more real than a hundred romances. Yet for many people this love remains a mystery, a dream, a fairy tale, a belief, but rarely a reality. How can you know God's love? How do you love a God you can't see, a God who is often silent, a God you can't touch?

Prayer is the experience of loving God. Prayer is the effort to receive, return, and enjoy God's love directly. Prayer isn't a good deed. Prayer isn't a religious duty. It isn't something that God needs us to perform. Nor is prayer a kind of Christian magic that allows us to control life's outcomes. Prayer is like spending time with a loving friend. Prayer is opening our hearts to the One who is the source of all love. Prayer is like lying in a field of falling snow. Silent. In wonder. Waiting until you hear the One who is closer than your own breathing whisper what your heart has always known to be true: That you are loved. That your value is incalculable. That you are cherished. That you are a sign of God's love in the world.

There are many ways to love God. We love God by loving what God loves. We love God by seeking to become the person God created us to be. We love God by sharing God's love with others, particularly the poor, the needy, those who are hurting or lonely. We love God by seeking to become like Jesus, by seeking to become a source of love and healing for others. We love God by becoming love. Like Jesus, we struggle to show kindness and hospitality to those who feel most unwanted.

One of the primary ways in which we share love with God is through prayer. We stop and turn our heart's eyes and ears to God. We stop and give our attention to God. We stop and spend time with the One who loves us into being.

∽

Scripture

Verses to draw your spirit to God...

Can a woman forget her nursing child,
or show no compassion for
the child of her womb?
Even these may forget,
yet I will never forget you.
See, I have inscribed you
on the palms of my hands.

ISAIAH 49:15-16

You are my child, my beloved,
with you I am well pleased.

MARK 1:11

For I am convinced that neither death, nor life, nor angels, nor rulers, nor things present, nor things to come, nor powers, nor height, nor depth, nor anything else in all creation, will be able to separate us from the love of God in Christ Jesus.

ROMANS 8:38-39

PRAYER

Words to help you speak to God...

O beloved of all hearts, how I yearn
to bask in your love!
To walk by faith rather than fear—
to be a companioning friend
to You.

For far too long I have felt unworthy,
like an orphan unwanted and alone,
forgetting that You call me by name;
You shelter me in the palm of
your hands!
Like all who open the heart's door,
You are mine, I am Yours!

O Beloved Friend, quiet my restless soul;
may I ever remember that my
true home is love.

NAN C. MERRILL

MEDITATION

Reflections to open your heart to God...

What keeps us alive, what allows us to endure?
I think it is the hope of loving, or being loved.
I heard a fable once about the sun going on a journey
to find its source, and how the moon wept without
her lover's warm gaze.

We weep when light does not reach our hearts.
We wither like fields if someone close does not rain
their kindness upon us.

MEISTER ECKHART

It is God's love that warms me in the sun
and God's love that sends the cold rain.
It is God's love that feeds me in the bread I eat
and God's love that feeds me also by
hunger and fasting.

It is the love of God that sends the winter days when
I am cold and sick, and the hot summer when I labor
and my clothes are full of sweat:
But it is God Who breathes on me with light winds off
the river and in the breezes
out of the wood.
His love spreads the shade of the sycamore
over my head.
It is God's love that speaks to me
in the birds and streams;
but also behind the clamor of the city...

and all these things are seeds sent to me
from God's will.

THOMAS MERTON

In the end we are judged by love.

JOHN OF THE CROSS

Contemplation

Exercises to help you spend time with God...

Breathing God's Love

Take a moment to set aside this book and lie down someplace where you'll feel comfortable and undisturbed.

For a few moments just notice your breathing. Every time you breathe in, imagine you're breathing in God's love. Every time you exhale, imagine you're releasing whatever fears, tensions, or doubts prevent you from receiving God's love.

For five minutes or more, let your prayer be an experience of taking in God's love and releasing all that hinders you from becoming love.

Notice what you're like after breathing this prayer. Then close by offering thanks to God for this time.

Sensing God's Love

Go sit in the sun, lie under the stars, put your feet in a cool stream, or (if it's cold) find a spot by a warm fire. Now imagine that you're experiencing God's love through your senses. If you are sitting outside on a sunny day, feel God's love in the warmth of the sun. If you're cooling your feet in a stream, imagine the cool water is God's love. If you're looking up at the stars, imagine the starlight is God's love shining down on you. If you're sitting next to a fire, imagine the warmth of the fire, the crackle of the logs, the golden firelight is God's love seeking to reach you. Let the wind, sun, rain, or light be God's love for you. Don't say anything, just rest and bask in God's love.

What is it like to experience these sensations as God's love? What is God's love like? What is prayer like when you just allow God to love you? After a few minutes you might talk to God, or take out a journal and write words to God, saying whatever comes to you.

Recalling God's Love

Ask God to remind you of a time when you felt deeply loved. Maybe it was when you were a child being held by a parent, or maybe it was spending time with a close friend. Maybe you were at an event with a group of people. Choose some experience when you felt deeply loved and appreciated. What was taking place? Where were you? How was this love shown to you? Were there words, gestures, or an act of some sort? How did you feel? Remember as much of the scene as you can. For the next few moments try to remember and savor the feeling of this experience of being loved.

Now, while you are still remembering this time, turn and ask God, "How were you present in this experience?" In silence, with your eyes closed, try to find the presence of God in this scene. In what way was God present? How did God love you in this experience? What words come to you as you recall God's love in this experience? What is your prayer?

Sources

Nan C. Merrill, *Meditations and Mandalas* (Continuum, 1999).

Meister Eckhart in *Love Poems from God*, Daniel Ladinsky, translator (Penguin, 2002).

Thomas Merton, *A Book of Hours*, Kathleen Deignan, editor (Sorin, 2007).

John of the Cross, *Meditations with John of the Cross*, Camille Campbell, translator (Bear & Co., 1989).

LONGING

CHAPTER TWO

As a deer longs for flowing streams,
so my soul longs for you, O God.

PSALM 42:1

A number of years ago I was preparing to go out of town for an important meeting. I was worried because my wife was feeling sick, and at the time we had two young boys who needed care. On the morning I was to fly out, I sat on the edge of our bed talking with my wife. My voice was taut with guilt and anxiety. My son Joseph, who was four years old at the time, heard my worried voice and walked into our bedroom.

"What's wrong?" he said.

"Mom's sick." I told him. "And Dad needs to go on a trip for a few days."

Joseph looked at his mom, then carefully walked over to the bed and gently placed his hand on her forehead. He closed his eyes and stood silent for a good minute. It was such a tender and curious gesture that, when he opened his eyes, I asked Joseph what he was doing.

"I was praying."

"And what did you pray?"

"I prayed that Mom would feel better."

"That's a very good prayer, Joseph. Mom needs our prayers." I reached down and hoisted him to my side. "Joseph, would you be willing to say a prayer for me, and my trip? I have to fly on a lot of planes. I would love to have you pray for me."

Joseph shrugged his shoulders, "Sure." He then placed his hand on my leg, closed his eyes, and sat in perfect silence. I closed my eyes as well, trying to receive the prayers of my son. After a moment or two he opened his eyes. I felt calmed.

"Thank you, Joseph." I said. Joseph turned to leave the room. "Hey, Joseph," I called after him. He stopped and turned around. "What did you pray when you prayed for me?"

Without hesitation he said, "I prayed for you to bring me a toy."

To be human is to yearn, to long, to hunger. In prayer and stillness we feel desire burning within us—desire for relationships, desire to create, desire to experience new things. Sometimes these desires burn in me like physical hunger—I want someone; I want to succeed; I want to be noticed. Desires can be messy and mixed up and even dangerous. And yet to be human is to yearn. To be human is to have yearnings and desires.

Joseph prays for a toy. Not because he's a materialist, but because he wants—he wants pleasure, delight, and the thrill of a new exciting object; or maybe because he wants to feel special, loved, and remembered by his father. As he grows older his restlessness will expand, multiply, become deeper and more complex. Sometimes his restless yearnings will become so turbulent in him that he won't be able to stand it. He'll work long hours, compose love letters, and stay up all night dreaming possibilities. Sometimes it will become so unbearable that he'll try to bury it. He'll try to distract himself—watch television, eat ice cream, stay busy, surf the Internet, keep the music blaring at all times...anything to avoid the ache of human longing.

Unfortunately, it often seems like advertisers are the only people who understand human desire.

On television, in magazines, on the Internet—advertisers work carefully to expose and misdirect our deepest desires toward brands, sexy people, food, material goods, and celebrities. Advertisers are wildly successful in helping most of us short-circuit our own simple yearnings, making us feel that if we only bought those shoes or owned that car or visited that resort, then we could be happy. Advertisers never suggest that the satisfaction to our yearnings is found in loving God and others. "Our hearts are restless until they rest in you, O God," Augustine noted within his own spiritual hunger. It is in prayer that we come to the root of our own restless yearning. It is in prayer that our true selves are coaxed out of hiding. It is in prayer that our hearts are uncovered, allowing our dreams, fantasies, and longings to be tended by God.

"What are you looking for?" Jesus asks a group of seekers (John 1:38). It's a powerful question. A question we often avoid. A question that can call up insatiable hungers, unmet hopes, broiling frustrations, dark impulses, and impossible dreams. Nevertheless, Jesus asks, "What are you looking for?"

When we pray, we're invited to face Jesus' question. We're invited to tend all the wants, longings, and desires that don't necessarily feel neat, and spiritual, and appropriate. And yet doesn't God welcome and even draw out these desires in us? Isn't it God's yearning for us that arouses our yearning for God?

Throughout the Bible we hear people bringing their desires to God. Prayer is Moses talking with God saying, "Show me your glory." Prayer is the author of the Song of Solomon pining, "Upon my bed at night I sought him whom my soul loves." Prayer is the Psalmist crying, "Do not hide your face from me." Prayer is Simeon and Anna waiting for a revelation within the temple. Prayer is the disciples of John the Baptist asking Jesus, "Where do you dwell?" Prayer is Zacchaeus climbing a tree, hoping the visiting teacher will show him a different way to live. Prayer is the hemorrhaging woman stretching to touch the hem of Jesus' cloak. Prayer is 12-year-old Jesus sneaking away from his family and running back to the temple in Jerusalem. Prayer is Jesus in the midst of his friends asking God to, "Make them one as we are one." Prayer is Jesus in the Garden of Gethsemane pleading, "If there is any other way…"

In the Bible we hear much of what resides within our own praying hearts. We want safety, we want insight, we want the truth, we want justice, we want to shout and dance and praise God in ecstasy, we want our tears and anger and suffering addressed, we want mercy and divine compassion, we want our enemies buried alive, we want to watch the rich and powerful suffer, we want to live forever with God. Despite the messiness of our yearnings, Jesus invites us to bring them to him. We're called to offer all that burns within our hearts to God.

And so we pray because we yearn. We pray because God wants us to reveal our hearts. We pray because God asks us to cry out our deepest longings. We pray because we trust that somewhere within these yearnings is the Holy Spirit, stirring up deep desires for life and truth and freedom and celebration and healing and relationship. We pray so we'll remember that our desires can't be satisfied by the world. We pray so we can channel these untamed desires to the only One who satisfies. We pray so we might find rest within our own burning hearts. We pray our desires to God so they might be guided, empowered, comforted, and accompanied even in the midst of the ache and longing of being human.

SCRIPTURE

Verses to draw your spirit to God...

"What are you looking for?"

JESUS, JOHN 1:38

"Ask, and it will be given you; search, and you will
find; knock, and the door will be opened for you.
For everyone who asks receives, and everyone who
searches finds, and for everyone who knocks, the door
will be opened."

JESUS, MATTHEW 7:7-8

O God, you are my God, I seek you,
my soul thirsts for you;
my flesh faints for you,
as in a dry and weary land where there
is no water.

PSALM 63:1

O Lord, all my longing is known to you;
my sighing is not hidden from you.

PSALM 38:9

Prayer

Words to speak your heart to God...

I give You these stirrings inside me,
I give You my discontent,
I give You my restlessness,
I give You my doubt,
I give You my despair,
I give You all the longings I hold inside.

THE NORTHUMBRIA COMMUNITY

You called, you cried, you shattered my deafness.
You sparkled, you blazed, you drove away
my blindness.
You shed your fragrance, and I drew in my breath,
and I pant for you.
I tasted and now I hunger and thirst.
You touched me, and now I burn with longing
for your peace.

AUGUSTINE

Meditation

Reflections to open your mind to God...

For I tell you this; one loving blind desire for God alone
is more valuable in itself, more pleasing to God and to
the saints, more beneficial to your own growth, and
more helpful to your friends, both living and dead, than
anything else you could do.

ANONYMOUS, THE CLOUD OF UNKNOWING

You have made us to be toward Yourself, O Lord, and
our hearts are restless until they rest in You.

AUGUSTINE

Like billowing clouds, like the incessant gurgle of the
brook, the longing of the soul can never be stilled. It is
this longing with which holy persons seek their work
from God.

HILDEGARD OF BINGEN

They came to Jericho. As he and his disciples and a
large crowd were leaving Jericho, Bartimaeus son of
Timaeus, a blind beggar, was sitting by the roadside.

When he heard that it was Jesus of Nazareth, he began
to shout out and say, "Jesus, Son of David, have mercy
on me!" Many sternly ordered him to be quiet, but he
cried out even more loudly. "Son of David, have mercy
on me!" Jesus stood still and said, "Call him here." And
they called the blind man, saying to him, "Take heart;
get up, he is calling you." So throwing off his cloak, he
sprang up and came to Jesus. Then Jesus said to him,
"What do you want me to do for you?" The blind man
said to him, "My teacher, let me see again." Jesus said to
him, "Go; your faith has made you well." Immediately he
regained his sight and followed him on the way.

MARK 10:46-52

CONTEMPLATION

Exercises to help you spend time with God...

What Are You Looking For?

Find a quiet place to pray. Take out a journal or a
piece of paper and a pencil. At the top of the page
write the question we hear Jesus ask a group of
seekers in the first chapter of John's gospel: "What
are you looking for?" Then take a few moments of
silence. Let yourself become aware of God's pres-

ence within and around you. After a moment or two, look at the question from Jesus, "What are you looking for?" and write out a response to this question. Don't worry about getting the grammar and spelling correct. Just let yourself write out all that you're feeling. What are you looking for at this moment in your life? Be honest. Tell Jesus the truth about what your heart desires.

Pray Your Heart's Desire

Find a photograph of yourself and hold it in your hands. As you begin the prayer, close your eyes and offer this time to God. Ask God to help you to pray the true desires of your heart. When you're ready, open your eyes and look at the photograph of yourself. Try to look at your image as if you were looking at a different person. Try not to judge or criticize the appearance of this person. See if you can look at yourself the way your mother or father or some other loving family member might look at you. After a few moments let this question come to you as you gaze at your own image in prayer: "What is this person's deepest wish?" or "What is this person's deepest longing?" Spend a few moments just holding this question in prayer. Don't try to force an answer, just see what God brings you in response to this question. Pray these longings to

God, and allow yourself to pray that God would respond to those deep longings. End the prayer by closing your eyes and holding the photograph to your heart. How is God responding to your deepest longings? Let yourself become aware of God's compassion for you as you rest in the silence.

God's Desire

Find a quiet, comfortable place to pray. If possible, light a candle to represent God's presence with you. Pray that you might become aware of God's desire for you. After a few moments read the following verse from the book of Micah:

> What does the Lord require of you but to do justice,
> and to love kindness,
> and to walk humbly with your God?

Spend a few moments talking with Jesus about God's desire for you. Ask Jesus, "How am I to embody justice?" Then wait in the silence. What images, faces, people, or actions come to you as you wait? Don't try to force anything. Just see what comes to you when you ask Jesus, "How do you want me to embody justice?"

After a few moments of reflection, ask Jesus, "How am I to love kindness?" Without forcing anything, see if there are words, images, or people that come to you in prayer when you wait and listen for how Jesus wants you to embody kindness.

Finally, ask Jesus, "How am I to walk humbly?" In what ways is Jesus asking you to embody humility? Wait and see what actions, images, or words come to you as you reflect on God's desire for you to become a person of humility.

Close your prayer by giving God whatever feelings, desires, fears, or doubts are residing in your heart. Then ask God to give you the strength and encouragement to embody justice, kindness, and humility.

Sources

The Northumbria Community, *Celtic Daily Prayer* (HarperOne, 2002).

St. Augustine of Hippo, *Confessions*, R.S. Pine-Coffin translator (Penguin Classics, 1961).

Anonymous, *The Cloud of Unknowing* (HarperOne, 2004).

Hildegard of Bingen, *Meditations with Hildegard of Bingen* (Bear & Co., 1983).

FEAR

CHAPTER THREE

"Peace I leave with you; my peace I give to you.
I do not give to you as the world gives.

Do not let your hearts be troubled,
and do not let them be afraid."

JESUS, JOHN 14:27

A few summers ago my sister Lisa and her husband, David, brought their kids out to visit us. The weather was hot and dry, so we decided to spend the first day at a lake. Siskiyou Lake is a popular place to swim in the summer and sure enough, when we arrived, the lakeside was crowded with sunbathers, swimmers, and picnickers. Within minutes my sons and young nephews had stripped to their bathing suits and were running and splashing in the clear mountain water. My brother-in-law, David, was also eager to swim and soon he was wading up to his knees, throwing a football to my sons while keeping his own two-year-old boy hoisted up on his shoulders. Meanwhile, I sat under an umbrella talking with my sister and watching her nine-month-old son carefully lick and swallow tiny tonguefuls of sand.

Suddenly, there was a cry—a voice from somewhere among the crowded swimmers screaming, "Help! Please help! Help!" The voice was urgent, terrified, and piercing.

Although I was about 60 yards from the water, I stood and scanned the shore until I located a boy's distressed face, tilted upward, barely above the waterline, fearfully screaming. I looked and watched as parents, other adults, and teenagers stood just a few feet away, watching in shock, watching in uncertainty, watching...and yet doing nothing to help the screaming boy. *Why wasn't anyone helping this kid?*

Then, from about twenty yards away, my six-foot-seven, 250-and-some-odd-pound brother-in-law started running. With white water exploding from his knees and his two-year-old son tucked under one arm, the big man crashed and splashed his way through the water. People jumped out of the way, parents pulled their children close to their sides, as David ran shouting, "Somebody help that kid! Somebody grab him!" But for some reason no one was willing to act. Instead, people looked at the boy or turned and looked at the big pale man violently crashing through the lakeshore.

They continued to stare as David, now waist deep, bent forward straining against the thick water, all the while yelling and pointing until finally he reached the frightened boy. He stretched out his one free arm, yanked the boy out of the water, and brought him tight against his chest. The boy, desperately relieved, wrapped both arms and legs around David's midsection and clung tight. David stood for a moment, allowing the boy to catch his breath. Then slowly, gently (his two-year-old still sideways under his other arm), David made his way to the beach and sat the boy in the sand. He knelt down and talked to the boy, making sure he was all right. There they waited together until the boy's parents showed up.

Life is scary. Human beings are small, fragile, and limited. Like the boy in the lake, my prayers often begin in fear or confusion—many of my prayers are some version of "Help me!" or "Have mercy on me!" Sometimes my prayers are so filled with my own worry and anxiety that I forget to stop talking and just listen to what God is doing. But when I do stop and listen, even though my prayer is filled with cravings and need and suffering and loneliness, I notice that God responds to me with rest and peace and love and comfort. I feel God wading through the waters, stretching out an arm and calling to me, "Hang on! I'm on the way!"

To pray is to be vulnerable. To pray is to seek God's care, guidance, encouragement, and peace—even when it feels ridiculous, when others look at us strangely, or when it feels like no one is listening or responding. Prayer is an act of trust; it's placing faith in the fact that God is real, that God is love, and that God responds to our cries. It's trusting—even when we feel like we're perishing—that God is with us, hears us, and cares about our need. It's trusting that, somehow God is making a way, even when we feel swallowed up in fear. In prayer, I learn to trust that God is moving through all the unfeeling, uncaring bystanders that live around and within me. Prayer is trusting, despite the present hurt and anxiety, that God hears me, holds me, and is gently working to bring me to dry land.

Have you ever seen small children cry when they're scared? Have you noticed when their parents come and hold them, they cry even harder at first, releasing all the hurt and fear? Eventually the cries slow down and get quieter and then at the end, just before the crying stops, the children take a deep breath and let out a long sigh, a release of all the tension and fear.

This is trust. This is what we're like in the presence of love. This is what it means to pray: We cry out (with fear or joy), we wait for the One who loves us, we allow ourselves to be held, we empty out our real fears and need (or our real joy and gratitude), and then we rest, knowing our lives are held in the hands of love.

SCRIPTURE

Verses to draw your spirit to God...

God is our refuge and strength,
a very present help in trouble.
Therefore we will not fear,
though the earth should change,
though the mountains shake in the
heart of the sea;
though the waters roar and foam,

though the mountains tremble with its tumult.
"Be still and know that I am God!"

PSALM 46:1-3, 10

Do not fear, for I have redeemed you;
I have called you by name, you are mine.
When you pass through the waters I will be with you;
and through the rivers, they shall not overwhelm you;
when you walk through fire you shall not be burned,
and the flame shall not consume you.
For I am the Lord your God,
the Holy One of Israel, your Savior.
...you are precious in my sight, and honored,
and I love you...

ISAIAH 43:1-3, 4

"Therefore I tell you, do not worry about your life, what
you will eat, or about your body, what you will wear. For
life is more than food, and the body more than clothing.
Consider the ravens: they neither sow nor reap, they
have neither storehouse nor barn, and yet God feeds
them. Of how much more value are you than the birds!
And can any of you by worrying add a single hour to
your span of life? If then you are not able to do so

small a thing as that, why do you worry about the rest? Consider the lilies, how they grow; they neither toil nor spin; yet I tell you, even Solomon in all his glory was not clothed like one of these. But if God so clothes the grass of the field, which is alive today and tomorrow is thrown into the oven, how much more will he clothe you—you of little faith! And do not keep striving for what you are to eat and what you are to drink, and do not keep worrying. For it is the nations of the world that strive after all these things, and your Father knows that you need them. Instead, strive for God's kingdom, and these things will be given to you as well."

JESUS, LUKE 12:22-31

"I will not leave you orphaned..."

JESUS, JOHN 14:18

PRAYER

Words to speak your heart to God...

"Abba...not what I want, but what you want."

JESUS, MARK 14:36

Lord, i will trust You,
help me to journey beyond the familiar
and into the unknown.
Give me faith to leave old ways
and break fresh ground with You.
Christ of the mysteries, can I trust You
to be stronger than each storm within me?
I believe You will make a way for me
And provide for me, if only I trust You.

THE NORTHUMBRIA COMMUNITY

MEDITATIONS

Reflections to open your mind to God...

Let nothing disturb you;
Let nothing make you afraid;
All things pass;
But God is unchanging.
Patience
is enough for everything.
You who have God
lack nothing.
God alone is sufficient.

TERESA OF AVILA

He became frightened, and beginning to sink, he cried
out, "Lord, save me!"
Jesus immediately reached out his hand and caught
him, saying to him,
"You of little faith, why did you doubt?"

MATTHEW 14:30-31

You will discover that the more love you can take
in and hold on to, the less fearful you will become.
You will speak more simply, more directly, and more
freely about what is important to you, without fear of
other people's reactions. You will also use fewer words,
trusting that you communicate your true self even
when you do not speak much. The more you come to
know yourself—spirit, mind, and body—as truly loved,
the freer you will be to proclaim the good news. That
is the freedom of the children of God.

HENRI NOUWEN

Above all, trust in the slow work of God.

PIERRE TEILHARD DE CHARDIN

CONTEMPLATION

Exercises to help you spend time with God...

Into Your Hands I Commit My Spirit

These words, "Into your hands I commit my spirit," were some of the last words Jesus spoke as he was dying (Luke 23:46). Even in the midst of violence, suffering, and death, Jesus was able to turn to God with trust and offer all that was within him. I find that these words give me a sense of peace and trust, reminding me that my heart, soul, and the very spirit of life within me belong to God.

Find a silent place to pray. Maybe it's on your bed at night or some quiet place outside. Now begin repeating Jesus' words—gently, prayerfully, in rhythm with your breathing. For example, as you breath inward you might say: "Into your hands..." Then, as you exhale, "I commit my spirit." In-breath, "Into your hands..." Out-breath, "I commit my spirit."

Continue to do this for five to ten minutes. Every time you get distracted or notice your mind wandering, just bring your focus back to your breathing, back to these words of Jesus, "Into your hands I commit my spirit."

Try to repeat these words throughout your day. You could draw a small cross on your hand to remind you to pray this line of Scripture. Every time you see this cross, just say within yourself, "Into your hands I commit my spirit." You might also try repeating these words every night before you go to sleep as a way of remembering that your life is held by God.

Over time, you'll find these words will come to you in times of distress or fear. If you continue to pray them, these words may help to quiet your heart and mind when you feel alone or anxious. These words of Jesus will help you embody the trust of Jesus.

Listening to God's Love for You

The following words from the first four verses of Isaiah 43 were words spoken by God to Israel. Fill your own name in the blank space, and read these words prayerfully, as if God is speaking them to you, just as God spoke them to the people of Israel.

But now thus says the Lord,
he who created you, O _____(your name)...

Do not fear; for I have redeemed you;
I have called you by name, you are mine.
When you pass through the waters
I will be with you;
and through the rivers,
they shall not overwhelm you;
when you walk through fire
you shall not be burned,
and the flame shall not consume you.
For I am the Lord your God,
the Holy One of Israel, your Savior…
you are precious in my sight, and honored,
and I love you.

What is it like to hear these words of God spoken to you? Does it bring you peace—or make you uncomfortable? When these words were written, water and fire represented the greatest fears of people. What are your greatest fears? What is it like to hear that God will be with you despite whatever terrors you encounter? Take a few moments and respond to these words in prayer. What is it you want to say to God when you hear these words addressed to you?

Praying Your Fear

This prayer invites you to pray with your fear. Before you begin, find a place to pray that is quiet and restful. This might be your bedroom, a quiet place in your home, or maybe someplace outside.

Begin the prayer by paying attention to your breathing. Every time you breathe in, imagine yourself breathing in God's love and life. Every time you breathe out, allow yourself to release whatever tension or distractions to God. Let this be a time of resting in God.

After a few moments of rest, let yourself feel the part of you that is afraid or fearful. Maybe you feel your fear as a tightness in your throat or a clenched feeling in your chest. As you notice your fearfulness, say within yourself, "Fear is present."

Now let yourself imagine that this fear is a young child. Let the fear be personified as a child. What does the child look like? What clothing is the child wearing? What expression does she or he have on her or his face? What is the posture of the child's body? Just let your imagination create an image of a child that represents your fear.

As you look or sense this child in your prayer, ask this question to the child, as if you were talking to a frightened child standing before you: "What are you afraid of?" Now wait and see how the child responds. Wait until you get a sense of why the child is scared.

Once you have some understanding of the child's fear, ask God's spirit to come and be with the child. Invite the Holy Spirit to come and be with this child in whatever way God wants. Maybe you notice God coming to the child as sunlight, or as a mother holding the child, or as a comforting song. Allow God to be with this child while you simply watch.

Now take a moment to receive whatever it is that God is trying to offer you through this prayer. Allow yourself to soak up whatever it is that God wants to give to you.

As this prayer comes to a close, notice any ways in which God is inviting you to respond to this prayer. Is there an action or new way of being that God wants you to embody as you leave this prayer? Then close by thanking God for whatever has occurred within your prayer.

Sources

The Northumbria Community, *Celtic Daily Prayer* (HarperOne, 2002).

Teresa of Avila, cited in Gerald May, *The Dark Night of the Soul* (HarperOne, 2005).

Henri Nouwen, *The Inner Voice of Love* (Image Books, 1999).

Pierre Teilhard de Chardin, "Above All, Trust in the Slow Work of God," cited by Margaret Guenther in *Pneuma*, Vol. 6, No. 2, Fall 1999.

SUFFERING

CHAPTER FOUR

Lord, have mercy.

MATTHEW 20:31

As you read these words, a child is suffering physical abuse from her father. As you hold this book, a man is weeping at the sudden loss of his wife. As you sit, a refugee is lying on a cot in North Africa trying to understand how she will survive without hands. As you reflect on these words, thousands of people feel despair at the addictions that enslave their bodies, the shame that fills their hearts, the thoughts of self-destruction that crowd their minds.

What do we do with senseless, meaningless suffering? This is the disturbing question that every human being has to live with. The world can be cruel. Innocent people suffer without cause—storms rise out of the ocean and drown the good and evil alike, cells mutate and cause cherub-faced children to deteriorate and die, parents abuse children, friends betray one another, and each of us struggles with his or her own particular darkness.

Suffering is as mysterious a reality as beauty or kindness. Like beauty and kindness, suffering can draw people close to God, yet it can also cause the most committed believer to lose all traces of faith. Suffering draws a person's soul to the surface. Suffering is where faith in God becomes real or disappears like a childhood daydream.

Through the Bible and the witness of the Christian community we learn that God wants to know our suffering. In prayer we discover that God is often found within our suffering, holding us with compassion, longing for the same healing and freedom we long for. In the midst of suffering God encourages us to cry out, to appeal for justice, and ask for mercy. The Bible encourages us to bring our deepest despair to God, to look for God within the darkness of our own pain and grief:

How long, O Lord?...
How long must I bear pain in my soul,
and have sorrow in my heart all day long?

PSALM 13:1-2

Turn to me and be gracious to me, for I am lonely and
afflicted. Relieve the troubles of my heart,
and bring me out of my distress.

PSALM 25:16-17

Give ear to my prayer...
My heart is in anguish within me,
the terrors of death have fallen upon me.

PSALM 55:1, 4

Hear my prayer, O Lord;
let my cry come to you...
For I eat ashes like bread,
and mingle tears with
my drink.

PSALM 102:1, 9

As a youth worker I remember a very bright and committed young woman in my youth group who struggled with an eating disorder. Eventually her condition became so disabling that she was hospitalized. One day I went to visit her in the hospital. Like many young women who suffer with anorexia, Diane was highly accomplished. She was an "A" student, an athlete, and the leader of many school clubs. She loved to spend her weekends working in various community service groups and was strongly committed to her church and her faith. Until Diane was hospitalized, she'd managed to keep her eating disorder a secret.

When I went to see her in the hospital, Diane was friendly toward me, but clearly was ashamed to be there. We made small talk for a while and then fell into a long, awkward silence. At a loss as to what to say, I asked if I could pray for her. Knowing she was a committed Christian, I asked how she was praying during this time. She told me she liked to pray with the Bible. I took out my Bible and asked if there were a particular verse I could read and pray with. Without hesitation she said, "Psalm 22." Tears came to my eyes as I realized that the words of despair Jesus turned to on the cross were the best expression of what this beautiful, capable, successful young woman was feeling.

I pulled a chair up to the bedside and read Psalm 22 while Diane lay with eyes closed. My tears fell over the pages as I came across verses like: "My God, My God, why have you forsaken me? Why are you so far from helping me?...O my God, I cry by day, but you do not answer; and by night, but find no rest...I am poured out like water...my hands and feet have shriveled, I can count all my bones...O Lord do not be far away! O my help, come quickly to my aid!"

No one suspected that this prayer resided in Diane, least of all me; and yet this was her secret prayer. It was within Diane's suffering that God called her to prayer.

Most of us have been trained to keep the agony and pain of our lives a secret. Ironically, churches seem particularly averse to human suffering. People dress up for church, greet one another with serene and pleasant faces, and keep things neat and orderly in worship. Church often feels like a place for pretending, a place for hiding all the mess and anguish of human living.

In the midst of suffering we need prayer. We need prayer in order to learn how to surrender, how to give up control, how to ask for help, and how to turn our lives over to the deeper reality of God's love. Often we find that our prayers grow out of suffering. We discover that prayer is the hope of suffering.

Our prayers are just pretending if we don't allow ourselves to give God the suffering we experience and witness in the world.

One way we endure and transform suffering is through prayer. Prayer allows us to penetrate the fear and pain we experience in this life and make contact with the Jesus who knows the burden and agony of human life. As we read the gospels, we notice that it is those who are suffering who make contact with Jesus—the blind, the lame, the hungry, the disoriented, the grieving, the lost and lonely. Jesus seeks out and befriends those who are suffering. He calls out to all who are hurting. With eyes of compassion, Jesus calls us to give our pain, our despair, our grief, and our hurt to him. Time after time, Christians discover that as we give our suffering to Jesus, even when the pain persists, in some mysterious, inexplicable way, it is enough. God's compassion is enough.

Scripture

Verses to draw your spirit to God...

> My God, my God, why have you forsaken me?
> Why are you so far from helping me, from the

words of my groaning?
O my God, I cry by day, but you do not answer;
and by night, but find no rest…
Do not be far from me,
for trouble is near
and there is no one to help.

PSALM 22:1-2, 11

How long will this pain go on, Lord,
this grief I can hardly bear?
How long will anguish grip me and agony wring my
mind?
Light up my eyes with your presence;
let me feel your love in my bones.
Keep me from losing myself in ignorance
and despair.
Teach me to be patient, Lord;
teach me to be endlessly patient.
Let me trust that your love enfolds me
when my heart feels desolate and dry.
I will sing to the Lord at all times,
even from the depths of pain.

PSALM 13 (ADAPTED BY STEPHEN MITCHELL)

He heals the brokenhearted,
and binds up their wounds.

PSALM 147:3

"Come to me, all you that are weary and are carrying
heavy burdens,
and I will give you rest.
Take my yoke upon you, and learn from me;
for I am gentle and humble in heart,
and you will find rest for your souls.
For my yoke is easy, and my burden is light."

JESUS, MATTHEW 11:28-30

Prayer

Words to speak your heart to God...

Sometimes I cry at night for all
I do not understand.
I feel so alone.
Then, as if in parents' arms,
or held in angel wings,
waves of love enfold me.
I think, "This must be the Friend,
the One I knew even before my birth."

Then my tears turn to smiles;
for I know I am not alone.
"Thank you," I whisper into the
silence of the night,
and sleep with peaceful heart
Until the dawning of a new day.

NAN C. MERRILL

Lord God, mercy is in your hands, pour me a little.

MARY OLIVER

MEDITATION

Reflections to open your mind to God...

When things are hard,
take refuge in Christ's heart.

MOTHER TERESA

"Blessed are the poor in spirit,
for theirs is the kingdom of heaven.

Blessed are those who mourn,
for they will be comforted.

Blessed are the meek,

for they will inherit the earth.

Blessed are those who hunger and thirst for
righteousness, for they will be filled.

Blessed are the merciful,
for they will receive mercy.

Blessed are the pure in heart,
for they will see God.

Blessed are the peacemakers,
for they will be called children of God.

Blessed are those who are persecuted for
righteousness' sake,
for theirs is the kingdom of heaven."

JESUS, MATTHEW 5:3-10

See, the home of God is among mortals,
He will dwell with them;
They will be his peoples,
and God himself will be with them;
he will wipe every tear from their eyes.
Death will be no more;
mourning and crying and pain will be no more
for the first things have passed away...
See, I am making all things new.

REVELATION 21:3-5

CONTEMPLATION

Exercises to help you spend time with God...

Here's an imaginative form of prayer that invites greater awareness of the places within us that wait for healing.

Find a safe, quiet place to pray. Get your Bible out and read the story of Jesus healing the paralytic in Mark 2:1-12.

Imagine God's love surrounding and holding you like warm sunlight. Notice your breathing, without altering it. Just imagine you are breathing in God's light and love.

Let your awareness move down into the core of your body. See if you can feel or sense a hurt for which you still need healing. Perhaps there's anger, fear, a sense of shame, or some other pain. How does this hurt live inside your body? Perhaps you feel an ache in your chest, a lump in your throat, a knot in your stomach, a pain in your forehead. Spend a few moments simply noticing this place that is in need of healing. Approach it with care and gentleness, as if you were approaching a hurt pet or child. If this part of you could speak, what might it say to you? Spend a few minutes listening to the words and feelings from this place of hurt. What does this place of hurt want to say to you?

Now imagine a group of people who love you—friends, family members, a pastor or teacher. Imagine these people have come to you just like the people who came to their paralyzed friend. Imagine these people who love you have lifted you up on a stretcher and are carrying you to Jesus. What do you feel, what do you hear, what do you see as you're being carried to Jesus?

Now, picture a crowd gathered within and around a small, simple house. Gently your friends carry you through the crowd until they stand at the outer wall of the house. Looking for a way in, they climb up onto the roof, then hoist you up above the crowd and onto the roof. Using their hands, they make an opening in the thatched roof. They smile at you, then gently lower you down through the roof—down into the cool darkness of the house, down until you rest on the floor at the feet of Jesus. The crowd is quiet. You can still feel the light from the sun coming through the hole in the roof.

You look up and see Jesus looking at you with compassion. What is it like to feel Jesus look at you in the midst of your own suffering?

Now imagine that Jesus reaches out and places his hand on you...maybe it's on the place in you that's in need of healing, maybe it's on your forehead or heart. For a few moments just allow Jesus to touch and pray for this place in you that needs healing. What is it like to have Jesus pray and care for this place in you? What are you like as you receive Jesus' love and compassion? Are there any insights, ideas, or actions that come to you as you receive Jesus' love and care?

Imagine Jesus helps you up from the floor. You turn and thank your friends, and then turn and thank Jesus for his prayer. Jesus invites you to come back to him any time to pray further about this place of hurt. You offer thanks to Jesus, and then turn and walk outside.

Close this time by spending a few moments offering thanks to God for whatever has occurred within your prayer, and then, if you want, journal your experience.

Healing a Hurt

This prayer invites you to open the painful moments in your life to God's healing. After finding a quiet, comfortable place to pray, spend a few moments becoming aware of God's presence with you. You might even sense that Jesus is next to you, praying with you. Offer this time to God in whatever way feels appropriate.

After a few moments, close your eyes and picture yourself in a sacred room within your own heart. The room is like a chapel lit with candles. In this room are images and objects that represent the deepest moments of your life. Some objects come from your childhood—pictures of loved ones, gifts given to you, things you played with as a child. You walk around the room noticing all the different symbols and objects that have shaped and formed your heart. Give yourself a few moments to be in this sacred space.

After exploring the different objects in the room, you notice that Jesus is standing next to you. He takes your hand and leads you to wooden box. As he opens the box, inside you see objects that symbolize past hurts and pain. He invites you to take one of these objects out. You're reluctant at first, but eventually you reach in and take out an image or object that represents a past injury. Jesus asks you to tell him how this hurt. For the next few moments tell Jesus all about it.

As you look up at Jesus, you see he is listening to you with care and compassion. Jesus then asks if he can hold this suffering for you. You reach out your hand and give it to him to hold. For the next few moments, notice what it's like to let Jesus hold this suffering for you.

After holding this wound, Jesus walks you to a small altar in the center of your heart. On that altar is a cross. Jesus lays your suffering on the altar then takes your hand and walks you out from the center of your heart, out into a green grass field and golden sunshine. You lie back on the grass and stare up at the blue sky. You feel the warmth of the sun on your face. And suddenly you feel light as air. For the next few moments, communicate to God the prayers of your heart.

When you're ready, offer thanks to God and close this time of prayer. If you have a journal, you may want to journal about this experience.

Images of Suffering

One way in which we heal the world is by being willing to see, feel, and hold the suffering in the world. Just as Jesus looked at and listened to lepers, grieving widows, lame and wounded people, so too are we called first to bear witness to the misery that is present in the world. It is in taking a long, loving, look at the real agony of the world that we uncover God's compassion and companionship.

One prayer exercise that invites us to really see, feel and hold the suffering in our world involves gazing and praying with pictures. Before you begin this prayer, find an image of suffering from a newspaper, magazine, or website. Maybe it's a picture of people suffering from hunger or war, a grieving mother who has lost her child, or a family of refugees who look worn and tired as they search for a home. Choose a picture that grabs your attention, a picture that somehow touches your own heart. Have this picture with you when you pray.

Find a comfortable, safe place to pray. Begin by asking God to open your eyes and heart to the suffering of others.

When you're ready, spend a few moments just gazing prayerfully at the image. What's happening in the picture? What are the various people experiencing? How would you respond if you were present to these people when this photo was taken?

What is the prayer of the people in your photo? Take a moment to hear their prayer. If you feel drawn to it, pray the words you imagine are being prayed by the people in your picture.

After seeking to be with the people in the picture, ask God, "How are you present in this experience?" Hold the picture in your hands. Let your hands represent the presence of God in this situation. What is it like to hold the people in the photograph in your hands? What is it like to feel this experience of suffering held by God?

Continue to reflect on God's presence within and beneath this suffering. Then ask, "God, what is your invitation to me as I look on these people?" You might want to have your journal available to write down what you sense God saying to you.

The Jesus Prayer

In the early days of the Christian faith (about 400 years after Jesus), there were people who fled the cities and towns to the wilderness in order to seek God. These early Christians, often referred to as the desert fathers and mothers, spent their lives seeking God in silence and prayer. Among the prayers these early Christians used was the prayer of the two blind men crying out to Jesus, "*Kyrie Eleison*" or "Lord, have mercy" (Matthew 20:31). They chose these words because they felt these words represent our fundamental relationship to God: We are people in need of God's mercy.

These early spiritual seekers would pray this prayer in rhythm with their breathing, seeking to move the words of this prayer into the very rhythms of their hearts until they found themselves praying "without ceasing." Although it's been modified into various forms over the centuries, the most common form of this "Jesus Prayer" is "Jesus Christ, Son of God, have mercy on me." Like the blind men who cried out to Jesus, when we offer this prayer we find a way to reach out to God in the midst of our suffering. If we continue to repeat this prayer through our daily life we find, like the desert mothers and fathers, a way to remain open to the one who is the source of all mercy and compassion.

Begin this prayer by asking the Holy Spirit to help you focus your mind and heart on the presence of Jesus. After a few moments of quiet, begin gently repeating the words of the Jesus Prayer, "Jesus Christ, Son of God, have mercy on me." Depending on your setting you can do this aloud, in gentle whispers, or just quietly within yourself. You might try this prayer while sitting, lying on your bed, or even while walking outside. Try to continue the prayer for at least ten minutes or longer.

You may notice as you repeat these words that you have a deep sense of prayer. The words start to become your own, expressing the real needs and desires of your own heart. Feel free to give your heart to Jesus as you pray these words.

The other thing you'll surely notice is that your mind gets easily distracted. Random thoughts, feelings, and memories will emerge, distracting you from your prayer. This is normal and happens to all of us who seek to pray. Don't worry if your mind wanders or drifts. Every time you notice your mind wandering, just go back to repeating the prayer, "Jesus Christ, Son of God, have mercy on me."

The early desert mothers and fathers believed that over time, as a person engaged the Jesus Prayer, the prayer would create a continual sense of God's presence. As we repeat the words, "Jesus, have mercy," we may have a growing sense that the prayer is no longer something we do, but instead has become who we are. At moments like this, the work of prayer ceases, and we find ourselves open, alive, and available to the spirit of Jesus.

Sources

Stephen Mitchell, *A Book of Psalms* (Harper Perennial, 1994).

Nan C. Merrill, *Meditations and Mandalas* (Continuum, 1999).

Mary Oliver, *Thirst* (Beacon, 2006).

Mother Teresa, *No Greater Love*, Becky Benenate & Joseph Durepos ed., (MJF Books, 1997).

COMPASSION

CHAPTER FIVE

When the Lord saw her, he had
compassion for her and said to her,
"Do not weep."

LUKE 7:13

M y family and I attend a small church in Southern
Oregon with a congregation of about 150 people.
Each Sunday about ten residents from a home for develop-
mentally disabled persons come and attend worship. Intel-
lectually, most of these people test at a first-grade level, but
their hearts and souls are big and beautiful.

During our worship service our pastor, Pam, invites people
to speak their prayer concerns out loud. This time is very tender as people ask prayers for ailing friends, troubled family
members, freedom from addictions, peace within war zones,

healing for the earth, and other heartfelt concerns. Most Sundays, Donald, a four-foot-ten, mentally handicapped man who is around 40 years old, speaks his prayers aloud. These prayers are often long, full of emotion, and difficult to understand. Sometimes we have to wait four or five minutes while Donald offers his heart in prayer.

A few Sundays ago our pastor was giving the church announcements before the start of the morning service as she does each week. Just as she finished, Donald stood, walked to the front of the church, and began to speak. His voice was shaky, and after a word or two he bowed his head and began to cry. Those who worship in our congregation each week are used to Donald's crying, and as I looked around the room I could tell that most people, like me, were eager for him to sit down so the service could begin. But instead of ushering him back to his seat, Pam walked over and stood by the crying man, patiently waiting for him to gain his composure.

After a few minutes Donald pulled himself together and held up a small photograph. He said, "This is a picture of me when I was 14 years old." He paused and held out the snapshot for all of us to see. We pretended to see the tiny images and smiled politely at Donald as if to say, "How nice…now let's get on with the service!"

Oblivious to our restlessness Donald pointed to a second figure in the photograph and said, "And that man is my dad." Again he paused and this time held the small 3 x 5 photograph over his head like a football fan with a sports placard. Again we smiled, then shifted in our chairs, irritated and eager for Pam to shuffle Donald to his seat. Yet Pam stood fully attentive to Donald's presentation. Then suddenly Donald dropped his arms, looked across the congregation, and in a clear voice announced, "My dad died last night." His words struck the room still. Then Donald's shoulders collapsed, his head sank, and he began to shake with grief. Gently Pam stepped over, wrapped her white robed arms around his body, drew his head to her shoulder, and let him weep.

For the next five minutes, maybe longer, Pam stood holding Donald, letting him cry as the rest of us sat staring. Watching Donald weep on Pam's shoulder, my frustration and impatience dissipated. Listening to Donald's cry, I could feel my own hurt and grief, my own need to be held with care and kindness. Watching Pam holding Donald, I quietly became aware of a deep sense of compassion growing inside of me—compassion for Donald, compassion for my own grief, compassion for all of us in that worship service who were afraid to stand up and let our tears be seen.

One of the fruits of prayer is that as we pray God begins to grow within us a greater sensitivity and compassion for suffering—the suffering of others, the suffering of the earth, the suffering within us, and the suffering of God. God is nothing if not a deep wellspring of compassion. We see this in Jesus as he offers kindness and care to the Roman soldier, the cheating taxman, the questioning prostitute, the sickly lepers, the hemorrhaging woman, the needy children, and the countless others he encounters. Jesus reveals to us that the deepest truth about God is that God feels an unrelenting compassion for human beings. To be a friend of Jesus is to share God's compassion with everyone we meet.

Prayer is a school of compassion, inviting us to spend time in the presence of a compassionate God so we might embody God's care for a broken world. Prayer by prayer we learn to carry a greater sense of caring and kindness. Prayer by prayer we learn to grow soft hearts, hearts that are transparent to the hurt that lives within the world.

We are all like the crying man in my church. Every human being—no matter how strong, how self-reliant, how cruel or cold—*every* human being is in need of God's compassion. Every human being wants to be heard; every human being wants to feel patiently embraced by other human beings.

It is equally true that we are all like my pastor Pam. Each of us has the capacity to care. Each of us has seeds of compassion within us, waiting to bloom and grow. Each of us has the capacity, with God's help, to hold what is ugly, frightening, broken, and unhealed in this world. Each of us is able, even now, to be the eyes of Jesus, the ears of Jesus, and the hands of Jesus for a world that often presents itself as cruel and unfeeling. In prayer each of us can make contact with that soft place within us where God dwells.

SCRIPTURE

Verses to draw your spirit to God...

When he saw the crowds,
he had compassion for them,
because they were harassed and helpless,
like sheep without a shepherd.

MATTHEW 9:36

"For I was hungry and you gave me food,
I was thirsty and you gave me something to drink,
I was a stranger and you welcomed me,
I was naked and you gave me clothing,
I was sick and you took care of me,
I was in prison and you visited me...
Truly I tell you,
just as you did it to one of the least of these
who are members of my family,
you did it to me."

JESUS, MATTHEW 25:35-36, 40

If I speak in the tongues of mortals and of angels, but do not have love, I am a noisy gong or a clanging cymbal. And if I have prophetic powers, and understand all mysteries and all knowledge, and if I have all faith, so as to remove mountains, but do not have love, I am nothing. If I give away all my possessions, and if I hand over my body so that I may boast, but do not have love, I gain nothing.

Love is patient; love is kind; love is not envious or boastful or arrogant or rude. It does not insist on its own way; it is not irritable or resentful; it does not rejoice in wrongdoing, but rejoices in the truth. It bears

all things, believes all things, hopes all things,
endures all things.

1 CORINTHIANS 13:1-7

PRAYER

Words to speak your heart to God...

Holy God,
Life is short,
and I do not have too much time
to gladden the hearts of
those who travel this life with me.
Help me to be swift to love,
and quick to be kind.

ANONYMOUS

Lord, make me an instrument of your peace;
Where there is hatred, let me sow love;
Where there is injury, pardon;
Where there is doubt, faith;
Where there is despair, hope;
Where there is darkness, light;
And where there is sadness, joy.

O Divine Master,
Grant that I may not so much seek to be consoled as
to console;
To be understood, as to understand;
To be loved, as to love;
For it is in giving that we receive;
It is in pardoning that we are pardoned;
And it is in dying that we are born to eternal life.
Amen.

ST. FRANCIS

MEDITATION

Reflections to open your mind to God...

My soul has a purpose, it is to love;
if I do not fulfill
my heart's vocation,
I suffer.

THOMAS AQUINAS

We have been created in order to love and to be loved.
It's possible that in the apartment or house across from
yours there is a blind man who would be thrilled if

you would go over and read the newspaper to him. It's possible that there is a family that needs something that seems insignificant to you, something as simple as having someone babysit their child for half an hour. There are so many little things that are so small many people almost forget about them. If you are really in love with Jesus, no matter how small your work, it will be done better; it will be wholehearted. Your work will prove your love.

MOTHER TERESA

In order to be of service to others, we have…to stop judging them, to stop evaluating them, and thus become free to be compassionate. Compassion can never coexist with judgment, because judgment creates the distance, the distinction, which prevents us from really being with the other. These judgments influence deeply [our] thoughts, words, and actions…Those whom we consider lazy, indifferent, hostile, or obnoxious we treat as such, forcing them to live up to our own views. These self-created limits prevent us from being available to people and shrivel our compassion.

HENRI NOUWEN

Just then a lawyer stood up to test Jesus. "Teacher," he said, "what must I do to inherit eternal life?" He said to him, "What is written in the law? What do you read there?" He answered "You shall love the Lord your God with all your heart, and with all your soul, and with all your strength, and with all your mind; and your neighbor as yourself." And he said to him, "You have given the right answer; do this, and you will live."

But wanting to justify himself, he asked Jesus, "And who is my neighbor?" Jesus replied, "A man was going down from Jerusalem to Jericho, and fell into the hands of robbers, who stripped him, beat him, and went away, leaving him half dead. Now by chance a priest was going down that road; and when he saw him, he passed by on the other side. So likewise a Levite, when he came to the place and saw him, passed by on the other side. But a Samaritan while traveling came near him; and when he saw him, he was moved with pity. He went to him and bandaged his wounds, having poured oil and wine on them. Then he put him on his own animal, brought him to an inn, and took care of him. The next day he took out two denarii, gave them to the innkeeper, and said, 'Take care of him; and when I come back, I will repay you whatever more you spend.' Which of these three, do you think, was a neighbor to the man who fell into the hands of the robbers?" He said, "The one who showed him mercy." Jesus said to him, "Go and do likewise."

LUKE 10:25-37

CONTEMPLATION

Exercises to help you spend time with God...

Nurturing Your Compassion

As Christians we know that we are supposed to care about others. Yet sometimes it can feel as if opening our hearts to someone else's pain and suffering is a duty, something forced. This exercise invites you to notice your capacity for compassion and allow God to expand it.

Begin by finding a quiet place to pray. Spend a few minutes just breathing, resting in the presence of God. After spending a few moments in silence, ask God to bring to your mind some moment in your past when you felt compassion for someone else. Maybe it was when you were a schoolchild, watching a classmate being picked on by other students. Or maybe it was in your home, feeling empathy for an injured sibling. Or maybe it was a more recent experience, feeling the hurt of a stranger in a newspaper or on television. Just allow God to bring you some moment when your heart felt the suffering of someone else.

Travel back to that place and time when your heart felt tender toward another human being. What did you see around you in that moment? What were the sounds? What was going on in your life at that time? Let the memory come to life.

Now see if you can recall the feelings. What does compassion feel like? For a few moments just recall the memory and allow yourself to draw up those feelings of compassion for another person. Let your body feel compassion.

When you're ready, invite God to come and be in that memory. Don't force or control anything—just invite God to enter into that memory. What do you notice? What is God's presence like?

After a few moments allow yourself to pray for the person in your memory. What is your wish for this person? Spend some time holding that person in prayer.

As you move toward the close of this prayer time, ask yourself this question, "What do I want to take with me from this prayer?" For a few moments see if there's a way God wants you to respond to this prayer. Then take a few moments just resting in silence with your heart still soft. Give thanks to God for this time of prayer, and make an effort to carry this soft, compassionate heart with you as you go about your day.

The more you remember these moments of compassion, the more you'll expand the tender places within your heart. Over time you might seek to bring more difficult people into your prayer and watch how God is inviting you to respond.

Practicing the Presence of Jesus

One way to carry prayer into your daily life is to try to practice the presence of Jesus throughout your daily activities. In the morning, before you start your day, draw a symbol on the back of your hand as a reminder of God's presence. Maybe it's a heart, or a word like "love" or "Jesus." As you go through your day, try to keep an ongoing sense that Jesus is walking with you in each moment, as if your closest friend were accompanying you throughout the day. Every time you notice the symbol on your hand, simply become aware of Jesus' presence with you. You might even say a simple prayer, something like, "Jesus, help me see you in this moment." What is your day like when you go through it with a sense of Jesus' companionship? What are other people like when you try to keep Jesus close?

Images of Blessing

Sometimes when praying for someone, it's helpful to picture that person in your prayer.

Close your eyes and picture someone who needs your prayers. Maybe it is a friend or someone who is sick or hurting. Maybe it is a group of people, such as civilians and troops suffering in a war, or people affected by a natural disaster. You might picture an enemy, someone with whom you're angry. If you are feeling a sense of self-loathing, you might picture yourself as the person in need of compassion. After a few moments of silence, picture this person surrounded by God's light. Without using words, simply see this person being healed and blessed by God's light and love. After a few moments of quiet, speak to God whatever words come to you.

In her nightly prayers, Teresa of Avila made a habit of remembering everyone she had seen that day. She would try to see each person in her imagination and then pictured herself placing her hand on that person's head and offering a blessing. Before you fall asleep, try going through your day picturing everyone you've encountered. Bless these people by touching each of them in your imagination—maybe with a hug, a touch of hands, or by placing a hand on their heads. See yourself blessing everyone you've encountered throughout the day, even strangers. What is it like to pray for people in this way? How do you feel about these people at the end of your prayer? See if you treat these people differently after blessing them with prayer.

The Prayer of St. Francis

Find the words from St. Francis printed in the prayer section earlier in this chapter. This familiar prayer, attributed to St. Francis, has been an inspiration to thousands of Christians who seek to live their lives as a blessing to others.

Take a few moments of silence to become aware of God's presence. When you're ready, read "The Prayer of St. Francis" as your own prayer. As you pray these words, notice any words that seem to stick out to you, the words that seem to be addressed to you. You might even circle or underline them. What is God trying to bring to your attention?

Now pray the prayer a second time. This time place your hands over your heart as you read it. Try to notice your feelings as you pray these words. What emotions is God bringing to your attention?

Now read it a third time. This time notice what names and or situations come to you as you read it.

Where do you encounter hatred, injury, doubt, despair? You might write down the names of people and situations where God's peace is needed.

Then take a moment to just sit and be with God in silence. What is God's invitation to you in these moments? How is God asking you to respond? You might take a few moments to write down your reflections.

Bringing Your Prayer to Others

Praying for others can be abstract when we only imagine those people in our minds. Our prayer is more real and rich when we can actually see, hear, and feel the people we pray for. Instead of praying for the sick from your bedroom, go to a hospital where you can sit in the waiting room and see the worried families, or stand outside the children's ward and see the children lying in bed. Instead of praying for the poor from your church sanctuary, go out to shelters, food banks, and the other parts of your community. Go out and pray within these places—pray for the people you see, touch, and hear.

I once took a group of students out to fields filled with migrant workers who spent their days bent over, harvesting fruit. The youth watched the backbreaking work these people did to provide food for others. We then went and prayed among the rundown and crowded apartments where these workers lived. After sitting, feeling, watching, and praying for these people, one young woman in our youth group asked if we might throw a Christmas party for the workers.

Three months later we rented a community hall near the fields and hosted a party for farm workers and their families. We had music, crafts, cookie making, and games for the children. At the end of the evening, youth group members gave the children Christmas presents that they had purchased and wrapped themselves. By going out of our church and into the lives of suffering people, not only were our hearts opened to the needs of others, we were also inspired to pray with our hands, our resources, our creativity, and our time. In a real sense we realized our prayer for these people was really God's prayer within us, calling us to act, to serve, to *become* prayer.

Sources

Thomas Aquinas in *Love Poems from God*, Daniel Ladinsky, translator (Penguin, 2002).

Mother Teresa, *No Greater Love* (New World Library, 2002).

Henri Nouwen, *The Way of the Heart* (Ballantine, 2003).

REST

CHAPTER SIX

"Learn from me…
and you will find rest for your souls."

JESUS, MATTHEW 11:29

Giving your heart time to pray is like allowing the sun to shine on wintering seeds. I notice that as I pray, my soul is slowly warmed and given room to expand, infused with God's peace and mercy. Prayer is the way in which I nurture and grow my life in God. Prayer is the way in which I hear Jesus calling from the center of my life, "Learn from me…and you will find rest for your soul."

The ancient understanding of the word *pray* within the Christian tradition is "to rest." Any experience of rest requires a release—we have to set down our work, our plans, our worry and activity. The fact that Jesus spent long periods of time resting is one of the most overlooked aspects of Jesus' life. He prayed and rested in the midst of suffering people. He prayed and rested in the midst of countless opportunities to do good.

Why did Jesus rest? Why did he withdraw from crowds of people desperate for healing? We know from Scripture that Jesus rested in order to commune with God. For Jesus (even Jesus!), prayer was necessary in order to sustain and deepen his capacity for love.

When we rest in prayer, we become open and receptive to God's presence. In the Christian tradition the experience of receiving God in prayer is called contemplation. Contemplation is an experience of being bathed in God's love and presence. It's an awareness of God, attained not through thinking but through loving. It is the experience Jesus refers to when he says, "abide in me" (John 15:4) or what the psalmist speaks of when he writes, "Be still and know" (Psalm 46:10). It's the experience the psalmist refers to when he describes a child resting on her mother's lap (Psalm 131:2). Contemplation in prayer is when suddenly we need no words, when we can relax and enjoy God's love with humility and gratitude.

I once took a bus full of high school kids to the coastal dunes two hours north of San Francisco. This diverse group of young people from across the country had gathered to spend the week exploring prayer. Midway through the week, we spent a day in the deserted Bodega dunes along the northern California coast. Amidst the rolling sand, native grasses, and twisting cypress trees, I talked to the students about the history of silence and solitude in the Christian tradition. I reminded them of the many times Jesus would leave people and towns to go out in the wilderness and spend time alone with God. I then asked the young people to go out along the sand and surf and spend the afternoon in prayer and solitude, just like Jesus did. As patches of fog drifted over us from the Pacific Ocean, I handed out journals and blankets and sent the young people out to pray.

I remember walking through the dunes carefully observing the praying teenagers. Some students sat atop mounds of sand, looking off to the horizon; others preferred low places, clefts and crevices stacked with driftwood. Some students lay on their backs, heads resting on their journals, watching grey shrouds of mist creep over the blue sky. Other students seemed oblivious to their surroundings, their heads bowed as they scribbled intently in their journals. As the hours passed, some people rolled themselves up in their blankets and closed their eyes, while others stood and meandered slowly toward the sea.

When the prayer time came to a close, I gathered the students together in small groups. "What was it like to pray?" I asked. "What were you like? What was God like?"

At the end of the week I asked the students to evaluate the weeklong retreat: "What was the most enjoyable aspect of our time together?" Despite game nights, talent shows, volleyball, karaoke, discussion groups, outings to San Francisco, and plenty of cute guys and girls to flirt with, the great majority responded, "The afternoon praying in the dunes along the beach." When I asked them why, they responded with, "I've never had that much unscheduled time before;" or "It was so peaceful to just rest with God;" or "My life is so stressful. I've never had time to just relax and be myself with God."

For years I've listened to people talk about their spiritual lives. One of the most interesting insights I've gained in these conversations is the way in which people describe their deepest encounters with God. Often these experiences of God are moments of rest, solitude, silence, reflection, and wonder. These encounters with God often take place as people lie on their beds at night, or in moments outside, in nature, looking at trees and earth and sky. Every one of these moments feels timeless, unscheduled, unhurried—as if they'd stepped out of the normal pace of their life.

Like the students who experienced an afternoon praying among the Bodega dunes, we may find that prayer offers us a release from the stress and busyness, the excessive activity that overwhelms each of us. Prayer gives us permission to loosen our shoulders, relax our jaws, and soften the walls around our hearts so God's love might make a way. Prayer is that increasingly rare opportunity to lie down in green pastures and rest beside still waters despite the fear and worry that we constantly feel.

Christians teach the message that "God loves you"—but this teaching means nothing unless we actually spend time in this love, unless we stop and kneel down in the grass and driftwood, down in the sand, down in the misery of a suffering world, down into God's compassion and peace.

SCRIPTURE

Verses to draw your spirit to God...

In six days the Lord made heaven and earth,
and on the seventh day he rested,
and was refreshed.

EXODUS 31:17

In returning and rest you shall be saved;
in quietness and in trust
shall be your strength.

ISAIAH 30:15

But now more than ever the word about Jesus spread
abroad; many crowds would gather to hear him
and to be cured of their diseases.
But he would withdraw to deserted places and pray.

LUKE 5:15-16

"Come away to a deserted place
all by yourselves and
rest a while."

JESUS, MARK 6:31

Prayer

Words to speak your heart to God…

Lord, when I sleep I feel you near.

MARY OLIVER

You are my shepherd,
I shall not want.
You make me lie down in green pastures;
You lead me beside still waters.
You restore my soul.

PSALM 23:1-3, ADAPTED

Meditation

Reflections to open your mind to God…

The sun hears the fields talking about effort
and the sun smiles, and whispers to me,
"Why don't the fields just rest, for
I am willing to do everything
to help them grow?"
Rest, my dears, in prayer.

CATHERINE OF SIENA

All shall be well, and all shall be well,
and all manner of things shall be well.

JULIAN OF NORWICH

"Come to me,
all you that are weary and
are carrying heavy burdens,
and I will give you rest."

JESUS, MATTHEW 11:28

CONTEMPLATION

Exercises to help you spend time with God...

Resting in God

When was the last time you allowed yourself to take a nap? What if you took some time to rest as prayer? Take a moment to withdraw from the busyness of your life. Find a quiet place where you won't be distracted. Then like the psalmist in Psalm 23, or the young people on the Bodega dunes, allow yourself to lie down.

Spend a few moments just allowing yourself to become aware of God's presence. One way to help yourself rest in God is to notice your breathing. For a few moments, let your breath be your prayer. Feel your body breathe in and breathe out. You don't need to say any words. Just let your breath be your prayer.

After a few moments repeat within you the following prayer, using words that Jesus used to address God, "Abba, I belong to you. Abba, I belong to you. Abba, I belong to you."[2] If you feel sleepy, allow yourself to close your eyes, with an awareness that you are resting in God's love. You might try this when you go to sleep at night, allowing a sense of God's peace to come over you as you fall into sleep.

Withdrawing

If we would stay close to our life in God, we all need retreat—some kind of withdrawal from our routines and hectic daily lives. The Bible tells us Jesus often withdrew to quiet and deserted places to pray. In many monastic communities bells are rung at various times throughout the day calling the members of the community to stop their activities, fall on their knees, and pray. I've been on retreat at a monastery where I watched men in kitchens, in fields, in gift stores and libraries suddenly stop their work, fall to their knees,

---

[2] I learned this prayer, "Abba, I belong to you," from Brennan Manning.

and open their hearts to God.[3] This ceasing of activity helps us gain perspective and keeps us in touch with the reality of God's life within and around us. Stopping is Sabbath-keeping. God's compassionate commandment frees us from our activity, so that we might receive and enjoy our life with God.

Spend some time "unplugged." Turn off televisions, computers, phones, music players, and video games. Then sit on your bed, lie in the grass outside, find a shady spot in a park, or hike into the nearest hills. Find a place where you are disconnected from entertainment, a place where no one can contact you, a place where you can just be with yourself and God. Bring nothing except a journal, a Bible, and a blanket. Then read, write, walk, pray, nap—just spend time in silence and solitude with God.

What is it like to be alone with God? What is it like to be without your gadgets? Does it make you anxious? Nervous? Is it a relief? Do you enjoy this time or dread it? The truth is that we came into this world alone and we leave this world alone. What is it like to be alone, with God? What is your prayer?

---

[3] For an experience of this kind of daily prayer see the documentary *Into Great Silence*. Set within a Trappist monastery high in the Alpine mountains in Switzerland, the film documents without soundtrack or commentary the silence and prayer these men seek to embody.

Silent Prayer

Many Christians find silence to be a deep experience of prayer. Silence can seem so awkward and strange at first, but if you look at your life you might notice you are actually quite familiar with silence. There are many moments in a day when we are quiet: Reading a book, riding a bus, sitting in the backyard, cruising the Internet, lying in bed at night, walking outside, skateboarding through the park, etc. In each of these moments we are silent. When are you silent during a day? What are these silences like? Have you ever walked away from friends, family, from home, from activity in order to get away from everyone and just think or pray or reflect on your life?

Next time you're in silence, listen for God—the way you might listen to a good friend who is sitting next to you. Brother Lawrence, a sixteenth century monk had a way of praying while he was working in silence. Every now and then, in the midst of his work and religious duties he would simply "glance" at God with the eyes of his heart, seeking to notice God's presence within the quiet spaces of his life. Next time you're walking or riding in a car or bus or some place alone or in silence, try looking at God with the eyes of your heart. Just notice God in the quiet. In the silent and unscheduled moments of your day, pause and allow God's presence to rise up within and around you. What are these silences like when you share them with God?

Centering Prayer

This form of prayer trusts the direct and immediate availability of God, the "indwelling Christ" who is nearer than our own heartbeat. We may think of prayer as thoughts or feelings about God expressed in words. But this is only one expression of prayer. Contemplative prayer is the full opening of mind and heart, soul, and body—one's whole being—to the Spirit of God, the ultimate mystery that is utterly beyond thoughts, words, images, and emotions. In contemplative prayer we open our awareness to the God who dwells within us—closer than breathing, closer than thinking, closer than choosing, closer than consciousness itself.

Centering prayer is a type of contemplative prayer in which we consent to the power of God's presence and unconditional love working within us. Here is one form of centering prayer based on the method devised by Thomas Keating.[4]

Sit comfortably in a prayerful space. Light a candle as a reminder of God's presence.

---

[4] This method of centering prayer is found in many of Keating's writings including *Open Mind, Open Heart* (Continuum, 1994) and *Centering Prayer in Daily Life and Ministry* (Continuum, 1998).

Choose a sacred word with which to pray. This word will be a symbol of your intention to be with God. This word expresses your desire to be in God's loving presence. Examples include *Jesus, Lord, Abba, Love, Mercy, Stillness, Faith, Trust, Shalom,* and *Amen.* Once you have selected a word, stick with it. Try not to get caught up worrying if some other word might be more "spiritual" and produce "better" results. Your word is simply a reminder of your desire to be with God. What's significant in this prayer is your intention (to be with God), not your particular word.

Before you start the prayer, close your eyes and settle yourself into God's presence. Allow yourself to feel a sense of warm hospitality, as if you were waiting to welcome a close friend or family member. Then begin silently introducing your sacred word as the symbol of your desire to know God's presence within and around you. Keating suggests you should say the word within you softly—"as gently as laying a feather on a piece of cotton."

It's important to remember that in silent prayer we will often experience our minds wandering into different thoughts, memories, and fantasies. It's not uncommon in centering prayer to forget we're even praying. Remember that this is an experience common to everyone who prays. The experience of prayer is very similar to the experience of listening to another person. Often when we try to listen to a good friend, our minds wander, we think of other things, we think of words we want to say, or we're distracted by things we see. It's the same in centering prayer; we try to direct our heart's attention to God, but often we find ourselves distracted. This doesn't mean we're not praying, it just means our minds are distracted. Every time you notice yourself feeling distracted, simply return to your word as a way of bringing your attention back to God.

After ten minutes or so, open your eyes and gently return your attention to the room. Close this prayer by giving thanks to God.

Sources

Catherine of Siena in *Love Poems from God*, Daniel Ladinsky, translator (Penguin, 2002).

Mary Oliver, *Thirst* (Beacon, 2006).

Julian of Norwich, *Enfolded in Love* (Darton, Longman, & Todd Ltd., 1980).

REFLECTION

CHAPTER SEVEN

I think of you on my bed, and meditate on
you in the watches of the night.

PSALM 63:6

Each summer when I was between the ages of 12 and 14,
my parents sent me to a three-week camp in Central California. Yosemite Sierra Summer Camp had all the elements
needed to awaken longing in a young person's heart. This
was classic summer camp—with tree-soaked air, heartfelt
singing, firelight stories, summer romances, lakeside sunsets,
quiet-time confessions, and the electricity of new friendships.
Because the camp was three weeks long, the daily schedule
was slow and relaxed, with time to play, sit outdoors, build
friendships, and for the first time, really reflect on my life.

Each camp session we were clustered in small groups of the same age and gender, and each group was assigned an adult counselor to befriend and guide us during our stay. For three weeks our counselor was our companion at every meal, recreational event, and worship gathering. He slept in our cabin, led evening devotions, answered our late-night questions, and pastored us through our different moods and difficulties.

I remember the last night of my final summer at camp. After ice-cream sundaes and counselor skits, Marcello brought us back to our cabin and with a somber face told us to dress warmly for a walk out to the woods. We dressed quietly, somehow sensing the need for a ritual on this final night. It was near 1:00 a.m. as we lined up outside our cabin, watching our breath rise like incense against the starlit night. Marcello came out, slowly looked at all of us, and then turned and walked toward the trees. With no need for instruction, we followed.

The camp was dark and shadowy, silent except for the crunch of our shoes shuffling on the graveled pathway. As we came to the edge of the forest, he stopped and asked us to sit on the pine-needled ground. I sat still and attentive, looking up at him, soaking in the import of this last night. In sparse sentences he told us we were leaving childhood. We were on our way to becoming adults. We would no longer be allowed to return to this camp. On this night it was important that each of us pray and reflect on our futures. What were our gifts? What were our weaknesses? Who was God calling us to be?

We were directed to stay at the edge of the forest and spend some time in prayerful reflection. He told us to try to see ourselves they way God sees us, then ask God to give us an image of the man God longed for each of us to be. Marcello looked reflectively at each of us, and then walked into a clearing about 50 yards away and sat on the largest stone among a cluster of boulders. I looked at my cabin mates. Instead of the smirks and goofiness that afflicted most of our gatherings, I saw them sitting with bowed heads earnestly following our counselor's direction.

I, too, lowered my head in my hands and, with eyes clenched tight, began to pray. I tried to see myself through God's eyes. I felt ashamed for the ways I treated my younger brother, and I could feel the way my teasing hurt him. I thought of the other kids at camp and felt remorse about the kids I'd made fun of, using them as a source of humor. I felt the goodness of my own desire to be kind, to live something beautiful for God. I then had an image of myself at that moment, sitting in the woods praying. I could feel God's compassion at the pain I was feeling over my parents' divorce. I sat, receiving this compassion, and then asked God to show me who I would become—who it was that God was forming me into.

Then Marcello began calling our names, one by one. I watched as each cabin mate rose and walked ceremoniously toward him. I noticed how Marcello looked at each boy, gently smiling, greeting each one with an embrace. I watched as each of my friends sat on one of the smaller stones. I stared as he spoke to them in a low whisper. Forgetting my prayer, I wondered what words he was imparting to them, and what he would say to me. Each time he finished speaking to a boy, Marcello returned to silent prayer until he called the next boy. I waited as he called one after another, until I was the only one left at the forest's edge.

Finally, he called my name. I felt awkward and self-conscious as I tried to walk unhurriedly to where he stood. I felt relieved as I looked at his warm and welcoming face. I sat next to him, and he asked what had come to me in prayer. I confessed the mean and often hurtful teasing I did to my brother and to others at camp. I talked about the pain of my parents' divorce. I talked about Jesus as a brave person, and how I, too, hoped to be brave. Marcello listened intently, and then in an intimate and intentional manner, he began to describe all the gifts he saw in me, all the moments when he'd sensed God alive in me. In prophetic phrasing, he began to tell me all the ways in which he saw me growing into manhood and all the attributes I was developing that would bring light to others. He then laid his hand on my head and prayed in simple words. He prayed for healing for the hurt I'd caused others and then thanked God for me, asking that I might become the man he saw me becoming.

That was the first time I remember being invited to stop and reflect prayerfully on my own life. Although it was nearly 30 years ago, the power of that self-examination is still with me today. I never saw Marcello after that 1979 summer camp, but I have clung to his words of forgiveness and blessing as if they were the words of a prophet. His words were the assurance that God was at work in me, a God who longs for me to live a full and abundant life.

All prayer is an invitation to self-reflection. We turn our attention to God, and in the light of God's love we notice faults and blemishes, we notice our soul's desires, we reconnect with repressed dreams, and we feel the pull of our strengths and gifts. Taking time to examine our lives in prayer isn't a psychological exercise. It's deeper than that. Prayerful self-reflection invites repentance, a turning from the ways in which we misdirect or misuse our lives, allowing God to heal and inspire us toward the person God created us to be. It's a time to notice and embrace our gifts, our skills, and the unique personalities God has given us. In a world full of distraction, it is prayerful reflection that can help us from being pulled by the sway of the culture, it is self-examination before God that keeps each of us close to his or her unique calling and vocation.

Scripture

Verses to draw your spirit to God...

O Lord, you have searched me and known me.
You know when I sit down and when I rise up;
you discern my thoughts from far away.
You search out my path and my lying down,
and are acquainted with all my ways.
Even before a word is on my tongue,
O Lord, you know it completely.
You hem me in, behind and before,
and lay your hand upon me.

Such knowledge is too wonderful for me;
it is so high that I cannot attain it.
Where can I go from you spirit?
Or where can I flee from your presence?
If I ascend to heaven, you are there;...
If I take the wings of the morning and settle at the
farthest limits of the sea,
even there your hand shall lead me,
and your right hand shall hold me fast.
If I say, "Surely the darkness shall cover me, and the
light around me become night,"
even the darkness is not dark to you; the night is as
bright as the day,
for darkness is as light to you.
For it was you who formed my inward parts;
you knit me together in my mother's womb.
I praise you, for I am fearfully
and wonderfully made.
Wonderful are your works; that I know very well.
My frame was not hidden from you, when I was being
made in secret,
intricately woven in the depths of the earth.
Your eyes beheld my unformed substance.
In your book were written all the days that were
formed for me, when none of them as yet existed.
How weighty to me are your thoughts, O God!

How vast is the sum of them!
I try to count them—
they are more than the sand;
I come to the end—I am still with you.

PSALM 139:1-18

You desire truth in the inward being;
therefore teach me wisdom in my secret heart.

PSALM 51:6

Prayer

Words to speak your heart to God...

O God, early in the morning I cry to you.
Help me to pray
And to concentrate my thoughts on you;
I cannot do this alone.
In me there is darkness,
But with you there is light;
I am lonely,
but you do not leave me;
I am feeble in heart,
but with you there is help;
I am restless,

but with you there is peace.
In me there is bitterness,
but with you there is patience;
I do not understand your ways,
but you know the way for me.

DIETRICH BONHOEFFER

God, give me grace to accept with serenity the things
that cannot be changed,
courage to change the things I can;
and wisdom to distinguish the one from the other.

REINHOLD NIEBUHR[5]

MEDITATION

Reflections to open your mind to God...

Why should I be anxious?
It is not up to me to think of myself.
It is up to me to think of God.
And it is up to God to think of me.

SIMONE WEIL

---

[5] For more on Reinhold Niebuhr and the history of the serenity prayer visit
http://skdesigns.com/internet/articles/prose/niebuhr/serenity_prayer/

My Lord God, I have no idea where I am going. I do
not see the road ahead of me. I cannot know for
certain where it will end. Nor do I really know myself
and the fact that I think that I am following Your will
does not mean that I am actually doing so. But I believe
that the desire to please You does in fact please You.
And I hope that I have that desire in all that I am doing.
I hope that I will never do anything apart from that
desire. And I know that if I do this, You will lead me
by the right road though I may know nothing about it.
Therefore will I trust You always though I may seem to
be lost and in the shadow of death. I will not fear, for
You are ever with me, and You will never leave me to
face my perils alone.

THOMAS MERTON

"The kingdom of God is among you."

JESUS, LUKE 17:21

CONTEMPLATION

Exercises to help you spend time with God...

Awareness Examen

The awareness examen helps us identify moments in our day-to-day lives when we are more open to God, others, and ourselves. These are moments of connection—moments when we feel more alive, more transparent to God, and more loving toward other people. It also helps us notice the opposite experience—moments when we feel disconnected, depleted, isolated, and cut off from the presence of God, others, or ourselves. As we consider our experiences, sometimes we notice patterns or occasions when we are in the flow of God's love; other times we see moments when we seem to be caught up in our own wounds and blindness. By paying attention to both kinds of moments in our lives, we become more aware of how our daily experiences can lead us toward or away from God.

Find a quiet place to pray. You may want to have a pen and journal. Take a few moments to relax and rest, gently becoming aware of God's presence, or the presence of Jesus, within and around you. Offer this time to God.

When you're ready, ask Jesus or the Holy Spirit to accompany you as you go over the previous day—from when you first woke up, to this moment right now. As you go through the day in prayer, allow this question to arise, "When was I most alive?" Allow little things to emerge: Talking with a friend, reading on your bed, eating pancakes, walking downtown. Choose one of these moments to meditate on. What does it have to teach you about your life with God? Don't force anything—just be open and let the moment arise that seems to hold the most life. You may want to journal your reflections. Now offer thanks to God for each of these moments.

Then, when you're ready, go back over the same day in prayer a second time. This time reflect on a different question, "When was I *least* alive today?" Allow God to bring your attention to whatever moment seemed most filled with disconnection, discouragement, a sense that God was absent: Arguing with a family member, over-eating, getting dressed in the morning. Take a few moments to prayerfully journal your prayer.

At the end of this prayer ask this question, "Jesus (or God), what is your invitation to me?"

This prayer can be very powerful if you do it each night before you go to sleep. Over time you'll notice patterns—moments when you are more open to God, moments when you are more closed to God. As you notice these patterns you'll see ways in which God is asking you to let go of certain activities, relationships, experiences, or behaviors, as well as ways in which God is encouraging you to increase other activities, relationships, experiences, and behaviors. Other questions you might use for this prayer include: When did I give and receive the most love? When did I give and receive the least love? When did I feel most free? When did I feel least free?[6]

Meditating on the Words of Jesus

Many of the questions Jesus asks in the Scriptures can bring us straight to our hearts. Below you'll find a list of questions Jesus speaks in the New Testament. You may want to choose a question that seems most interesting or attractive to you for this prayer. Or you might just choose a question randomly and see what happens in your prayer. Once you have a question from Jesus, find a place to pray. Continue to repeat the question until you feel you have given your deepest response.

Sometimes it's helpful to write out a conversation between you and Jesus. Take out a journal or

---

[6] These questions come from *Sleeping with Bread*, Dennis Linn, Sheila Fabricant Linn & Matthew Linn, (Paulist Press, 1995).

other writing materials. Write your name on one half of the paper and "Jesus" on the other half of the paper. Then write out a conversation between you and Jesus. Start with Jesus asking you a question from the list below. Remember this is prayer, not a writing assignment, so take some time to sit in silence after you read the question, then write down what comes to your heart as you imagine Jesus asking this question of you, right now, today. Allow a conversation to develop.

Here's a selection of questions that Jesus asks in the New Testament:

Why do you see the speck in your neighbor's eye, but do not notice the log in your own eye?

MATTHEW 7:3

Why are you afraid?

MATTHEW 8:26

Why did you doubt?

MATTHEW 14:31

Are your hearts hardened?

MARK 8:17

Do you have eyes, and fail to see?
Do you have ears, and fail to hear?

MARK 8:18

Who do you say that I am?

MARK 8:29

Why do you call me "Lord, Lord,"
and do not do what I tell you?

LUKE 6:46

Where is your faith?

LUKE 8:25

What does it profit you if you gain the whole world,
but lose yourself?

LUKE 9:25

Can any of you by worrying add a single hour to your
span of life?

LUKE 12:25

What is the kingdom of God like?

LUKE 13:18

What do you want me to do for you?

LUKE 18:41

Do you want to be made well?

JOHN 5:6

Do you love me more than these?

JOHN 21:15

Praying with Colors

Sometimes words get in the way of prayer. Our word-based prayers can become repetitive and stuck; other times we find it difficult to pray and don't know what to say. Sometimes we get a greater sense of our own life in God when we pray without words. This prayer invites you to pray with colors, opening yourself so that God might meet you in a new way, through images and creativity.

Find some paper and a handful of crayons (or marking pens, colored pencils, etc.) and go to a place where you can pray undisturbed. Take a few moments to quietly ask God to be with you and to reveal to you your own heart.

Then, when you're ready, prayerfully ask God or Jesus, "What is my life with you like on this day?" Let yourself draw, in prayer, using whatever images or colors seem to come to you. Maybe you have a particular image that comes to you, or maybe you have something more abstract—yellow and blue swirls, smeared red and orange blotches. Whatever it is, allow God to be with you as you pray.

When your drawing is finished, you might reflect on these questions in prayer: What am I like when I pray this way? What is God like in this prayer? What is God trying to bring to my attention in this prayer? You might close this prayer by turning to God and asking, "God what is your invitation to me?"

This same kind of prayer can be done with other creative media as well. Try praying with clay, watercolors, charcoal and paper, or finger paints. See if you discover a new awareness of God and your own life when you pray without using words.

Breakfast with Jesus

Take out your Bible and read John 21:1-14, the story of Jesus' resurrection appearance to the disciples on the Sea of Tiberias. In this story we find Jesus sitting on the beach grilling fish and bread for his friends, the disciples. In this prayer you're invited to imagine yourself on that beach, eating and talking with Jesus.

Begin by closing your eyes and imagining yourself breathing in God's light and love. With every out breath, allow yourself to let go of any distractions, tension, or anxiety that is within or around you.

After a few minutes of quiet, open your eyes and read the following. Allow yourself to imagine yourself within the biblical story. You may want to first read the exercise below and then just close your eyes and imagine yourself going through the story in one sitting, or you may want to pray the exercise as you read it. Every time you see , let yourself pause and imagine the story in prayer.

Imagine yourself sitting in the sand, on the edge of a sea. It's morning, the air is brisk, and the sun is glistening on the water. You smell the salty air mixed with the faint smoke of a fire with grilled fish and bread. You look up and down the coastline. It's open, vacant except for a small group of friends eating and conversing around a fire made of driftwood and charcoal. You watch this group and see that the people seem relaxed and happy. They laugh easily and seem to be enjoying themselves.

You continue to watch this group on the beach until you notice one man in particular. He's looking at you. His eyes are soft. He notices you sitting by yourself and gestures for you to come over. He holds a piece of bread in the air, offering it to you. You immediately feel hungry and want to accept the man's invitation, but for some reason you stay seated and shake your head "no." The man with the soft eyes smiles at you knowingly. You turn and look out across the sea.

While looking out to the horizon you hear footsteps moving through the sand and hear a voice next to you say, "Here, I've brought you some food." You look over and see the man with the soft eyes. Immediately, you know this is Jesus. He sits next to you, and you're surprised how comfortable you feel with him. You accept the food gratefully and notice how good it is not to be alone. Both of you sit quietly for a while. Then Jesus turns and says to you, "So tell me. How are you?"

For the next few minutes allow yourself to honestly respond to Jesus and his question, either through journaling or just within your own heart.

Now, as you close this time of prayer, take a few moments to let Jesus respond. Feel free to journal his response or just listen to what takes place within your own heart.

Sources

Dietrich Bonhoeffer, *Letters and Papers from Prison* (Touchstone, 1997).

Rienhold Niebuhr, *The Essential Reinhold Niebuhr* (Yale University, 1987).

Simone Weil in Dorothee Soelle, *The Silent Cry* (Augsburg Fortress, 2001).

Thomas Merton, *Thoughts in Solitude* (Farrar, Straus, and Giroux, 1999).

PASSION

CHAPTER EIGHT

Do not neglect the gift that is in you.

I TIMOTHY 4:14

S even days after Christmas, I was eating breakfast in the Portland International Airport. The terminal was crowded; the mood post-holiday hectic. I was seated in a kind of lounge, a large atrium with glass windows that rose two stories high overlooking the tarmac. In the middle of this open lounge sat a large grand piano. The piano had a black cover and a laminated sign that read: "Please do not remove cover or play piano. For professional use only. Thank you. —PDX Airport."

Fifty yards from where I sat were the zig-zag lines of the airport's largest security checkpoint. As I sipped coffee, a frazzled looking couple with two kids came walking through the security detectors. Each parent held a young child while frantically rummaging through various diaper bags and backpacks. As they approached, I could hear them arguing. At one point the woman shouted, "I don't know where it is! I just know I packed it!" The father set down his three-year-old daughter and began to search through his jacket pockets. The toddler was wearing special shoes that made an erratic, high-pitched, squeak-toy sound. This gave the girl great pleasure. Smiling, she stomped her feet around her parents with a "Squeak! Step. Step. Squeak! Step. Squeak! Step. Squeak! Squeak!"

"Those shoes are going to make me insane!" the man said threateningly. He snatched his daughter from the floor, yanked the shoes from her feet, and set her back down. Various people around me looked at one another with raised eyebrows while the little girl stood and hung her head.

Then there was a scream. A young man was shouting, hollering in fear within the glass examination room at the center of the inspection line. People from all over the atrium turned and stared as two red-faced security guards tried to frisk a confused and frightened mentally handicapped man. While the man screamed in terror, a heavyset woman in a purple sweatshirt banged her hand against the Plexiglas and called in to the guards, "You're scaring him! He doesn't understand!"

The noise set everyone on edge, particularly the security guards who were now talking animatedly into their walkie-talkies as their supervisors scurried toward the shouting voices. Travelers from all across the airport stopped and stared, transfixed by the escalating chaos.

Suddenly, from somewhere among the bystanders, a Hispanic boy around the age of 16, wearing baggy jeans and a hooded sweatshirt, walked out into the middle of the lounge area. He picked up the sign from atop the grand piano, set it on the floor, pulled back the black cover, adjusted the bench, set his fingers on the keys, and began to play. The music was so beautiful that at first I was certain it was a recording piped in through the airport sound system. It was a classical piece, with a lush, lilting melody.

With eyes closed, the boy swayed back and forth, weaving the notes amidst the frightened yelling, the frantic hustle of travelers, and the blaring announcements from the airport intercom. On and on the boy played, and people gradually quieted and drew closer to him. Some turned their chairs to face the piano. Others picked up their trays and bags and walked over to get a better listen. A server from the coffee stand came out to clear tables and then noticed the boy at the piano. She stopped her work, smiled at me, and said, "It's Mozart."

On my right, the arguing parents were now sitting on the floor, still rummaging through bags. As they sat, their shoeless daughter heard the music and, trancelike, wandered slowly into the open space beside the piano. She stood for a moment, taking in the music. Then gingerly, spontaneously, she began to dance the primal fairy dance known by all three-year-old girls. With arms flung wide, she twirled, pranced in circles, and from time to time made tiny, delicate, fairy-leaps.

The mentally handicapped man, his face still red with tears, came over from the security lines, barged into the edge of the gathering audience, and stared at the piano. His eyebrows furrowed in concentration as he watched the little girl dance. His female companion soon joined him, looking harried and spent. Then she took in the scene for a moment, wrapped her arms around the man, and sighed. Within moments the handicapped man was swaying and laughing without worry.

A group of National Guardsmen walked over to a cluster of chairs at the edge of the seating area. They were dressed in military fatigues, readying themselves for departure. From the faces of their wives and children, it was clear they were leaving for a long deployment. Most of the women looked distressed, their hands reaching often to touch the arms of their husbands.

Then a young man, looking like a college student—with glasses, torn jeans, white earphones, and a backpack—walked over to the piano. He carefully set down his bags, opened a violin case, moved behind the piano player, and placed the violin to his chin. The student waited and listened for a moment, then began to play a supporting harmony. The Hispanic boy, eyes still closed, hands still moving across the keys, simply smiled as if to say, "Yes. This is what happens…"

For the first few moments the violinist played softly; then the piano quieted into a series of chords. Right on cue, the violinist stepped forward and lifted up the melody with the heart tones of his instrument. He knew the piece well and soon the sound of his strings was echoing throughout the concourse. Smiles broke out among us at this beautiful surprise, and some onlookers began to applaud.

A little boy about the same age as the dancing girl appeared from among the group of National Guardsmen. He was dressed in camouflage military fatigues that matched his father's. Captured by the music and the dancing toddler girl, he walked out onto the open floor and began to make his own careful circles, arms waving up and down like a bird. His mother spotted him and strode abruptly onto the floor, quickly hoisting the boy back to her side. Moments later, the boy slipped away from his mother, stepped out into the open space, and resumed his quiet little dance. Again the mother noticed him, became embarrassed, and moved to gather him in. But this time her husband stopped her. Seeing his son dancing, the father's face filled with emotion. He turned to his wife and shook his head for her to let it be. The mother looked at her husband and was startled by his wet eyes. The soldier then picked up his chair, moved away from his comrades, sat down, and watched his young son dance. Soon his wife came over and stood behind him wiping her own tears from the corners of her eyes.

When the music came to an end, there was a grateful burst of applause. The boy at the piano smiled and stood, then turned and shook hands with the violinist. An elderly woman, eager to show her gratitude, walked over and placed a dollar on the piano. This touched something in the audience and soon many of us were digging bills from our bags and wallets. Meanwhile the violinist briskly packed his instrument and backpack with the urgency of someone who needs to catch a plane. He shook the pianist's hand a second time, waved at the smiling audience, and started to make his way out. A man grabbed his shoulder and pointed to the pile of money, fifty dollars or more, waiting at the edge of the piano. The young man looked at the money, grinned widely, sheepishly looked around at all of us watching, and then shook his head "No." He then bowed and strode off to his gate.

All of us turned to the piano player, to see if he would take the money. But when we looked, he was gone. The elderly woman who had placed the first dollar on the piano lifted her arms and shouted, "Where's that beautiful piano boy?" All of us shrugged our shoulders, then with mild awkwardness, retrieved our little bills and went our separate ways. As I hurried toward my gate, a woman walking next to me in business attire with briefcase in hand, said, "Now, *that* was Christmas."

The crowd that gathered there had a sense of being in the presence of something sacred, something miraculous and alive as we watched and listened. Those two young men who played music in the Portland airport had a gift. A gift for music, obviously—but also a gift that blessed people, drew out kindness in people, made us feel more alive, more human. It was clear that music is the passion of each these young men. Music is their calling, the unique way in which they carry and express the beauty of God.

God has made each of us to embody and reflect the light of God. The God who knit us together in our mother's womb (Psalm 139:13) created each of us with a particular gift, a particular way of being, and a unique purpose God longs for us to carry out into the world. This calling, this way of being, is our passion. This calling is the way in which we feel full of purpose, full of life, full of meaning, at home in our own lives.

Part of our life's work is to seek out, discover, celebrate, and develop our passions. Like hand-cut glass, each of us shines God's light in fresh, original, and significant ways. As we live, our restless spirits encourage us to learn new things, explore different identities, participate in various activities, and engage various communities. Like a piece of glass held up to the light, each of us struggles to find the angle, the way of living that best reflects the light of God. Each of us struggles to find and claim a life that best reflects the person God created us to be. We are all looking for our passion, our purpose, the way of being in the world that makes us most transparent to God and others.

Sometimes we're born knowing our passion—like a child who sits mesmerized at a piano, feeling her spirit awake and alive, calling excitedly to her mother, "I'm going to be a piano player!" Sometimes we search and struggle for years. I have friends who didn't really discover their passions until well into their forties. It's difficult to hear your own calling, your own passion, amidst so many voices (the culture, your parents, friends, teachers) telling us who we should be, what we should care about, how we should live.

One of the gifts of prayer is that in prayer we can sometimes feel the way God has created us to be. In prayer we can come back home to who we are and feel the Spirit affirming us in who we are (no matter how strange or different from others), encouraging us to claim our gifts and live them out in the world. Our passions, our callings, are gifts from God.

How do you find your passion? Well, sometimes it takes some living to discover it, but there are always signs: What stories or movies are you attracted to? What experiences in your life would you most like to repeat? Whom do you most admire? What do your friends say is unique about you? What activities do you get absorbed in and lose track of time? What would you do if you had the time and money to do anything? If you had only one year to live, what would you do?[7]

Our passions, our gifts, don't have to be what others tell us. Nor do they have to be "artistic." Your passion might be a way of being with people, a way of thinking, or a way of seeing the world. My brother-in-law Jack has a passion for finance. His eyes fill with light as he talks about helping people fund their homes, their business ideas, or their hopes for their children. Jack's passion, just like that of the musicians in the airport, is a blessing to others. My friend Kirk has a passion for language. He pays attention to the words in songs, in books, in conversation. He creates and collects beautiful images and phrases and shares these with his students.

---

[7] Most of these questions were taken from or inspired by questions in *Healing the Purpose of Your Life* by Dennis Linn, Sheila Fabricant Linn, and Matthew Linn (Paulist Press, 1999).

What is your passion? How is God encouraging you to come alive? What are your gifts? What is the unique way in which God has made you? The prayers in this chapter invite you to reflect on your gifts, claim your passion, and trust that you have a particular purpose that bears God into the world. In the Christian faith, we are commonly called to pray our sins, our faults, our brokenness and shortcomings. But for God to shine through us into the world, we need to claim the passions God has asked us to embody. (Sometimes this can be more difficult and painful than confessing our sins.)

May each of us feel as blessed and gifted as the two young musicians in the Portland airport. May each of us live out our passions without shame, no matter how discouraging those around us might be. As Macrina Wiederkehr, a Benedictine sister, once prayed,

O God,
help me to believe
the truth about myself
no matter
how beautiful it is![8]

[8] *Seasons of Your Heart: Prayers and Reflections* (HarperCollins, 1991).

Scripture

Verses to draw your spirit to God...

Before I formed you in the womb
I knew you,
and before you were born
I consecrated you...

JEREMIAH 1:5

"I came that they might have life, and
have it abundantly."

JESUS, JOHN 10:10

Now there are varieties of gifts,
but the same Spirit;
and there are varieties of services,
but the same Lord;
and there are varieties of activities,
but it is the same God who activates all of them in
everyone.
To each is given the manifestation of the Spirit
for the common good.

1 CORINTHIANS 12:4-7

Prayer

Words to speak your heart to God...

I want to free what waits within me
so that what no one has dared to wish for
may for once spring clear without my contriving.

If this is arrogant, God, forgive me,
but this is what I need to say.
May what I do flow from me like a river,
no forcing and no holding back,
the way it is with children.

RAINER MARIA RILKE

God be in my head,
and in my understanding;
God be in my eyes,
and in my looking;
God be in my mouth,
and in my speaking;
God be in my heart,
and in my thinking;
God be at my end,
and at my departing.

THE SARUM PRIMER

MEDITATION

Reflections to open your mind to God...

Live your life like a work of art.

ABRAHAM HESCHEL

The glory of God is manifest in the person fully alive.

IRANAEUS OF LYON

The place God calls you is where your deep gladness
and the world's deep hunger meet.

FREDRICK BEUCHNER

The real difficulty about prayer is that it has no
difficulty. Prayer is God's taking possession of us.
We expose to Him what we are, and he gazes on
us with the creative eye of Holy Love. God's gaze is
transforming: God does not leave us in our poverty
but draws into being all we are meant to become.

SISTER WENDY BECKETT

CONTEMPLATION

Exercises to help you spend time with God...

Sealed Orders

A Christian writer named Agnes Sanford once wrote that God gives every human being "sealed orders."[9] These sealed orders are the unique way of being and special purpose that God has given each of us to live out in the world. This prayer invites you to reflect on your gifts, your passion, the unique way of being God wants you to embody in the world.[10]

Find a quiet place to pray. Begin by breathing in God's love.

When you're ready, imagine yourself with God, before you were born. What do you see around you? What do you hear in this place? Take a moment to imagine yourself, before you were born, dwelling in the presence of God.

Now, imagine that you and God have been discussing the special purpose of your life and you have agreed to it. Your purpose is a way of being in the world that feels natural and right to who you

---

[9] Agnes Sanford, *Sealed Orders* (Logos International, 1972).

[10] This prayer is based on a healing exercise in *Healing the Purpose of Your Life*, Dennis Linn, Sheila Fabricant Linn, and Matthew Linn (Paulist Press, 1999) p. 34.

are. At the end of the conversation, God hands you an envelope containing your sealed orders. You open the envelope and see what is inside.

Take a few moments to experience what is inside the envelope. Is it a picture, a feeling, a memory, a word, an idea? Spend a few moments reflecting on how God has made you to live in the world.

Now take a moment to recall good friends, loving family members, mentors, and others who know you well. What do these people say they like about you? How do they reflect back to you the special purpose, the unique way of giving and receiving love, that God has given you to live out in the world?

What is God trying to offer you in this prayer? Take a few moments to take in whatever it is that God wants to give to you in this prayer.

As your prayer comes to a close, consider whether there is some invitation to act—some way God is asking you to respond after praying this prayer. Take a few moments to see if there is something God wants you to remember or do as a result of this prayer.

Close the prayer by offering thanks to God. You may want to journal whatever has come to you or share the insights from this prayer with a trusted friend.

Being Yourself

Jesus often went outdoors when he needed to return to who he was and the way in which God loved him. He would walk to the edge of a lake or sometimes go up high on a mountain. Other times he would look for a quiet, deserted place in the wilderness. Is there a place in nature where you feel most inspired, most cared for, most like yourself?

Pack a backpack with a journal and some crayons or colored pencils. Bring water and some good snacks and spend an afternoon out in the natural world. Go someplace where you feel alive and comforted, someplace where you feel most like yourself—however you are. A wise monk once said, "A tree praises God by being a tree." When you're out in nature notice how everything reflects God by just being itself: Grass being grass, stones being stones, birds being birds. Spend a few moments just looking around you noticing how everything is peacefully being itself. Let yourself draw comfort and inspiration from this place.

Then, in prayer, reflect on this question, "What is the unique way I was created to give and receive love in this world?" You may want to write that question on a piece of paper before you spend some time sitting quietly in prayer. When you're ready, let yourself respond to this question in whatever way you choose. Maybe lots of words will come to you; maybe some picture or image comes; maybe an idea will come to you. Let yourself respond in whatever way seems most natural. Then from time to time, when you feel lost or disconnected from your own heart, return to this setting and notice the plants, the earth, and the creatures—and then reflect, once again, on how God has created you to give and receive love in this world.

Open Hands

Find a place to pray that is quiet and private, where you'll be undisturbed. Find a comfortable seated position—maybe sitting crosslegged on the floor or with your back against a wall, or maybe it's in a chair with your feet on the ground and your back straight. After getting comfortable, close your eyes and place your hands on your lap with your fingers curled in (like a fist).

Just spend a few moments noticing what it's like to be in the presence of God with your hands closed. What do you notice? What feelings arise? What parts of you are closed? What is God like in the midst of the parts of you that are closed up?

After a few minutes of silence, slowly roll out your fingers until your hands are fully open. Now spend a few minutes noticing what it's like to be in the presence of God with your hands open. What is it like to be open before God? What are you like, what is the world like, when your hands are open? After four or five minutes, talk to God about what you're feeling. What is your passion? What kind of person is God inviting you to be in the world?

God Be In Me

Find a place to pray where you'll be undisturbed and lie down on your back. Take a few moments just to notice your breathing. When you've settled into prayer, offer yourself and this time to God.

When you're ready, place your hands on the top of your head and say either out loud, or within yourself, "God be in my mind and in my understanding." Pause for a moment and see what you notice.

Then place your hands on your ears and say (either out loud or within yourself), "God be in my ears and in my hearing." Again pause and see what you notice.

Now place your hands on your eyes and say, "God be in my eyes and in my seeing." Pause for a moment and see what you notice.

Bring your hands to your mouth and say, "God be in my mouth and in my speaking." Pause to see what you notice.

Now place your hands over your chest so you can feel your chest rising and falling with your breathing. Now say either aloud or within yourself, "God be in my breath and in my living." Notice what comes to you in the silence.

Finally, place your hands over your heart and say, "God be in my heart and in my loving." Take a moment to see what you notice while your hands rest over your heart.

Now repeat these movements in silence, gently moving your hands from head to ears to eyes to mouth to chest to heart. Feel free to stop for a while if there's one place on your body that seems to call you into deeper prayer.

After a while, offer whatever you've noticed to God in your prayer, and then gently close your time by giving thanks to God for your body and your life.

Sources

Rainer Maria Rilke, *Rilke's Book of Hours: Love Poems to God*, Anita Barrows and Joanna Macy, trans. (Riverhead, 1997).

Sister Wendy Beckett, *The Gaze of Love* (Harper San Francisco, 1994).

WONDER

CHAPTER NINE

The people who walked in darkness
have seen a great light.

ISAIAH 9:2

The wise Rabbi Abraham Heschel once wrote, "Prayer is our humble answer to the inconceivable surprise of living." *The inconceivable surprise of living.* God is trying to awaken the soul of every person so we might experience life fully. God wants to increase our sensitivity to the world so we see, hear, and feel more of life. In every moment God yearns for us to see and recognize God's beauty and love.

When I was five years old, my grandfather, Monroe Freeman, hitched his round, silver dollar trailer to his truck and drove me up to the San Bernardino Mountains. It was springtime, the clover was blooming, and my grandfather, a weekend beekeeper, needed to collect honey. In silence we drove from freeway to rural highway to mountain lane to dirt road until finally my grandfather, whom I affectionately called "Popo," rambled the truck off into a mountainside meadow. He parked the truck in a field of clover and instructed me to stay inside, out of the bright sun. Then he walked a few hundred yards to a stack of white wooden boxes that looked like an abandoned wedding cake sitting among the clover.

I sat on the musty, quilted bed and felt the warm Southern California wind that gently swirled the sweet smell of clover blossoms in and through the trailer doors. A few times I sat up and looked out across the meadow to watch my grandfather. Dressed in a white cloak and veiled hat, he moved slowly and deliberately among the tiny black bees, swinging a small smoking canister like an Easter priest processing incense through the congregation.

Restless, I jumped up and down on the springless bed, then sat on the steps of the trailer, then returned to jumping. Seduced by the sun and green hillside, and against my grandfather's instructions, I stepped out of the trailer. Without any particular destination I tromped through the waist-high clover, running my hands over the tiny blossoms.

At some point, I felt a tiny vibration tickle my hand. Startled, I stopped and noticed a cluster of round flowers attended by a sisterhood of gold-and-black-coated bees. It was fascinating to watch their dark, thorny legs high-step through the soft mustard carpet of each flower. Wanting a closer look, I knelt down to bring my eyes level with the working bees. I don't know how long I stayed kneeling among the clover; I do know the moment felt eternal—the warm summer wind, the gently swaying field, the bees delicately moving from blossom to blossom. I knelt in timeless wonder while a warm contentment moved through my body, like being embraced from the inside out.

My grandfather came up behind me hauling a five-gallon bucket heavy with honeycombs. "Are you praying?" he asked playfully. I stood quickly, worried I was in trouble for leaving the trailer. Popo's hat was unveiled and cocked back on his head. Smiling, he reached down. "Here. Try this." He handed me a small melting glob of honey. I placed it in my mouth. It was warm, surprisingly thick, and filled my whole mouth with sweetness. "It's wax in the middle, so don't swallow it."

I chewed carefully, sucking out the little pores of liquid flowers, until I had a chewing gum wad of wax. "What were you doing out here?" My grandfather asked, setting the bucket beside me.

I looked at him tentatively, still wondering if he was upset. "Looking at bees," I said.

He nodded his head, reached down to hand me another soft shard of honeycomb, and said gently, "Well, it seemed like you were praying."

All throughout my growing up, I would reflect on this moment among the bees and clover. I had felt the edge of something, something mysterious and wonderful, some secret wholeness, something beyond the reach of my own mind, something holy and eternal, some kind of beauty at the center of the shimmering world. It's only now—now that I'm in my forties, now that my grandfather has passed away, now that the clover field has been leveled and paved into a housing development, now that 70 percent of the wild honeybees have disappeared from North America—that I can finally give a reply to my grandfather's question.

"Yes, you were right. I was praying."

To be a follower of Jesus means to live with a certain kind of awe, amazement, and wonder at the life God has given us to live. And yet how are we to develop a sense of wonder if we are rarely given the space and permission to gaze at the world around us? How can we experience the joy and surprise of living if life is presented as something to be mapped out, planned, and accomplished?

Shouldn't Christians be constantly falling to our knees in gratitude at the beauty of the rising sun, the pleasure of good food, the simple gift of warmth and friendship, and all the other miracles of life? Why is it only when we get cancer or someone close to us dies that we start to look at the world and realize how beautiful and wonderful it is? Why is it only when death is close that we feel so grateful to be alive?

When was the last time you felt a sense of awe or wonder? When was the last time you sensed the miracle of life, the beauty of being alive, the wonder of love, and the mystery of God's presence in the world (and in you)? To pray is to slow down— to step out of the busyness and distractions and remember that life is a gift. To pray is to be in wonder at what God has created. To pray is to be in wonder at God. To pray is to enter into the mystery of this life, a mystery to which we can only respond with prayer, with awe, with stunned silence, with fumbling words. As Mechthild of Magdeburg, a Christian mystic from the 13th century once wrote: "Of the heavenly things God has shown me, I can speak but a little word, no more than a honeybee can carry away on its foot from an overflowing jar."[11]

SCRIPTURE

Verses to draw your spirit to God...

Amazement seized all of them,
and they glorified God
and were filled
with awe.

LUKE 5:26

My God, how great you are!
Beautifully, gloriously robed,
Dressed up in sunshine,
and all heaven stretched out for your tent.
You built your palace on the ocean deeps,
made a chariot out of clouds and took off
on wind-wings.

---

[11] Stephen Mitchell, ed. *The Enlightened Heart* (HarperCollins, 1993).

You commandeered winds as messengers,
appointed fire and flame as ambassadors.
You set earth on a firm foundation…
You blanketed earth with ocean,
covered the mountains with deep waters…
then you roared and the water ran away—
your thunder crash put it to flight.
Mountains pushed up, valleys spread out
in the places you assigned them.
You started the springs and rivers,
sent them flowing among the hills.
All the wild animals now drink their fill,
wild donkeys quench their thirst.
Along the riverbanks the birds build nests,
ravens make their voices heard.
You water the mountains from your heavenly
cisterns…
You make grass grow for the livestock,
hay for the animals that plow the ground….

Mountain goats climb about the cliffs;
badgers burrow among the rocks.
The moon keeps track of the seasons,
the sun is in charge of each day.
When it's dark and night takes over,
all the forest creatures come out…

What a wildly wonderful world, GOD!
You made it all, with Wisdom at your side,
made earth overflow with your wonderful creations.
Oh, look—the deep, wide sea,
brimming with fish past counting,
sardines and sharks and salmon....
You come, and they gather around;
you open your hand and they eat from it.
If you turned your back,
they'd die in a minute—
Take back your Spirit and they die,
revert to original mud;

Send out your Spirit and they spring to life—
the whole countryside in bloom and blossom....

Oh, let me sing...all my life long,
sing hymns to my God as long as I live!

PSALM 104, THE MESSAGE

On that day, when evening had come, he said to them,
"Let us go across to the other side." And leaving the
crowd behind, they took him with them in the boat,
just as he was. Other boats were with him. A great
windstorm arose, and the waves beat into the boat, so
that the boat was already being swamped. But he was

in the stern, asleep on the cushion; and they woke him up and said to him, "Teacher, do you not care that we are perishing?" He woke up and rebuked the wind, and said to the sea, "Peace! Be still!" Then the wind ceased, and there was a dead calm. He said to them, "Why are you afraid? Have you still no faith?" And they were filled with great awe and said to one another, "Who then is this, that even the wind and the sea obey him?"

MARK 4:35-41

PRAYER

Words to speak your heart to God...

Holy Friend,
Help me to sit here a moment
and sense your gaze
and the wonder
of your silent love.
Amen.

THE IRISH JESUITS

The Canticle of Brother Sun

Most High, all-powerful, all-good Lord,
All praise is Yours, all glory, honor and blessings.
To you alone, Most High, do they belong;
no mortal lips are worthy to pronounce Your Name.
We praise You, Lord, for all Your creatures,
especially for Brother Sun,
who is the day through whom You give us light.
And he is beautiful and radiant with great splendor,
of You Most High, he bears your likeness.
We praise You, Lord, for Sister Moon and the stars,
in the heavens you have made them bright, precious and fair.
We praise You, Lord, for Brothers Wind and Air, fair and
stormy, all weather's moods,
by which You cherish all that You have made.
We praise You, Lord, for Sister Water,
so useful, humble, precious and pure.
We praise You, Lord, for Brother Fire,
through whom You light the night.
He is beautiful, playful, robust, and strong.
We praise You, Lord, for Sister Earth,
who sustains us
with her fruits, colored flowers, and herbs.
We praise You, Lord, for those who pardon,
for love of You bear sickness and trial.

Blessed are those who endure in peace,
by You Most High, they will be crowned.
We praise You, Lord, for Sister Death,
from whom no-one living can escape.
Blessed are those that She finds doing Your Will,
No second death can do them harm.
We praise and bless You, Lord, and give You thanks, and
serve You in all humility.

FRANCIS OF ASSISI

Meditation

Reflections to open your mind to God...

When we say "God is eternal," we mean:
God is eternally young;
God is ever green, ever verdant, ever flowering.
Every action of God is new,
for he makes all things new.
God is the newest thing there is;
the youngest thing there is.
God is the beginning
and if we are united to him
we become new again.

MEISTER ECKHART

The Summer Day

Who made the world?
Who made the swan, and the black bear?
Who made the grasshopper?
This grasshopper, I mean—
the one who has flung herself out of the grass,
the one who is eating sugar out of my hand,
who is moving her jaws back and forth instead of up and down—
who is gazing around with her enormous and complicated eyes.
Now she lifts her pale forearms and thoroughly washes her face.
Now she snaps her wings open, and floats away.
I don't know exactly what a prayer is.
I do know how to pay attention, how to fall down
into the grass, how to kneel down in the grass,
how to be idle and blessed, how to stroll through the fields,
which is what I have been doing all day.
Tell me, what else should I have done?
Doesn't everything die at last, and too soon?
Tell me, what is it you plan to do
with your one wild and precious life?

MARY OLIVER

When he came to Nazareth, where he had been
brought up, he went to the synagogue on the Sabbath
day, as was his custom. He stood up to read, and the
scroll of the prophet Isaiah was given to him.
He unrolled the scroll and found the place where it
was written:

"The Spirit of the Lord is upon me,
because he has anointed me
to bring good news to the poor.
He has sent me to proclaim release to the captives
and recovery of sight to the blind,
to let the oppressed go free,
to proclaim the year of the Lord's favor."

And he rolled up the scroll, gave it back to the
attendant, and sat down. The eyes of all in the
synagogue were fixed on him. Then he began to say
to them, "Today this scripture has been fulfilled in your
hearing." All spoke well of him and were amazed at the
gracious words that came from his mouth.

LUKE 4:16-22

CONTEMPLATION

Exercises to help you spend time with God...

Finding God in the Little Things

Jesus often found that objects in nature reflected the presence and wonder of God. Trees, birds, flowers, grass—as Jesus looked at these natural objects he saw signs and symbols of God's presence in the world. This prayer invites you to find an object that draws you into prayer and reflection.

Find a place outside where you can walk as you pray. Offer this time to God. You might want to ask Jesus or the Holy Spirit to go with you in this prayer, asking God to open your eyes, ears, heart, and mind to God's truth and love.

As you begin this prayer, notice your surroundings. Notice all God has made. If you're in a natural setting, notice the wind, the trees, the birds and their sounds. If you're in a city or neighborhood, notice the plants, the buildings, the streets and sidewalks—all of this comes from the world God has created. As you take in your surroundings, notice what you hear. Notice what you see. Notice how you are feeling.

When you're ready, prayerfully walk and explore your surroundings. Notice what God is bringing to your attention. When something catches your attention—a plant, a stone, a blade of grass, a bird, whatever it is—allow yourself to stop, maybe even sit, and just be with whatever part of your surroundings God is asking you to notice. Don't force anything, just simply listen and look for a part of nature that seems to call for your attention.

Like Jesus, allow yourself to meditate with this object. What is God saying to you as you pray with this small piece of the world? Notice what thoughts, feelings, and images come to you as you reflect on this object. What is being offered to you?

When you're ready, express yourself in some way to God. Pray whatever feelings, desires, requests, or gratitudes have come to you in the prayer. Communicate your honest thoughts and feelings to Jesus or God until there is nothing left to share.

After a few minutes, simply rest in God. Bask in whatever God has given you in this prayer. Allow yourself to rest in the midst of what God has created. Allow yourself to drop beneath all your thoughts and feelings and rest in the God who loves the whole world into being.

If possible, you might want to take this object back to your home to remind you of your prayer. Or you might take out your journal and sketch the object or just simply journal your prayer.

Each time you walk outside, try to notice what attracts you and draws your attention. See if the world can become more and more lit up with the presence of God.

Praying Wonder

Recall an experience of wonder, some moment when you were filled with awe and amazement. Maybe it was a moment outside, some experience of natural beauty, or maybe it was a moment with other people—watching a child, enjoying the wisdom of a grandparent, listening to a piece of music played in a café. If you're having trouble, ask God to bring to mind some experience of wonder. Then wait for it to arise.

Allow yourself to recall this experience in as much detail as possible. Travel back to those moments, as if you were a time-traveler going back to that space and time in your own history. Recall the details of the experience: What did you see, what did you hear, what did you feel like in that moment of awe and wonder? You may want to try to draw or write about this experience to help you enter it more fully. Let a sense of awe return to you. Then, when you're ready, allow this question to arise in your prayer: "God, how were you present in this experience?" See what comes to you in silence as you reflect on this question. Maybe an image comes that you'll want to try to draw or color. Maybe words come that you'll want to write out. Or maybe there is a feeling, idea, or intuition that rises up in you. Try to sense how God was present in this experience of wonder. Dwell in this presence for a few moments.

As the prayer comes to a close, ask God, "What is your invitation to me?" See if God is inviting you to respond in some way to whatever you have experienced within your prayer. Then close by offering thanks to God for whatever you've recalled within your prayer.

An Image of God

We know God is a mystery. The Bible tells us not to create idols of God, because God cannot be contained by our words, thoughts, or images. And yet, at the same time God gives us many images to help us get a sense of who God is. In the Bible we find many images of God: Water, mother eagle, loving father, wise mother, bread, light, and more. This prayer invites you to seek an image that will help you grow closer to God.

As you begin this prayer, close your eyes and rest for a while, just allowing yourself to become aware of God's presence within and around you. After a few moments of quiet, ask God to give you a symbol or image of God. Don't try to force anything, just allow the Spirit of God to form an image within you that helps you grow in your love for God. Be open to whatever God brings you in prayer. It may be a color, a natural image like the ocean, a tree, or a rose. It may be a sense of light or water, or it may be a person, a face, either familiar or unfamiliar. See if you can receive this image as a sign of God's presence with you. What is it like to have this image of God? What is God like as you pray with this image? What feelings arise in you? Take some time to draw or write about this image in your journal.

Another way to do this prayer is to choose an image from the Bible that expands your heart—some image of God that comforts you. Look through the Psalms and choose an image. Spend some time just holding this image within you as a symbol of God's presence. What do you notice as you pray with this image from the Bible? What is God like? What is

God's call to you as you pray with an image of God as cloud, burning bush, loving father, mother eagle, or some other biblical image?

Sources

The Irish Jesuits, www.sacredspace.org.

Francis of Assisi, www.prayerfoundation.org.

Meister Eckhart, *Meditations with Meister Eckhart*, Matthew Fox, ed. (Bear & Company, 1982).

Mary Oliver, *House of Light* (Beacon Press, 1990).

GRATITUDE

CHAPTER TEN

I will give thanks to the Lord with my
whole heart.

PSALM 111:1

"If the only prayer you say in your entire life is, 'Thank you,'
that would suffice," Meister Eckhart once said. All true prayer
carries a spirit of gratitude. When we pray we say to God,
"Thank you for my life. Thank you for your presence. Thank
you for being God."

It is good to give God thanks, not only because God has giv-
en us so much, but perhaps more importantly because of what
gratitude does to us. It's hard to be anxious when you're grateful. It's difficult to keep your guard up, to be cold and defended
when you're overcome with thankfulness. Prayers of gratitude
open the gates of the heart so God's love can enter in.

Much of the real suffering in this life is because we don't know how to receive the gifts of God, let alone the presence and love of God. We spend most of our days preoccupied, caught up in our own anxious worry. Most days we walk past the ten thousand gifts God offers us—warm sunlight, the pleasure of nature's colors, the smell and taste of good food, the warmth of friendship, the comfort of sleep. Even in difficult times these gifts of love and presence come to each of us a hundred times a day—and yet, we rarely see them, rarely take them in, rarely take the time to receive the God who comes to us in a constant stream of graces.

Our lives are a gift. Our faith is unearned. Our prayer is given to us with no strings attached. Why does God give us, as ungrateful as we are, so many pleasures, so many graces, so many delights? I don't know. What I do know is that there is joy in giving to someone you love. What I do know is that when we gratefully receive God and God's way of life, we give God pleasure. What I do know is that in gratitude we become more alive, more free, and better able to love others.

When my next-door neighbor Priscilla was diagnosed with cancer, the doctors told her she would die within a year. Priscilla was in her early fifties.

Her son was just starting college, and her daughter was about to graduate from high school. The family was shattered by the news. Priscilla quit her job, tried alternative medicines, visited various doctors, and underwent various operations, but nothing seemed to work. Within months she began to accept that her life would soon end.

I remember how I'd often see Priscilla in the mornings when I'd go out to my driveway as my sons and I prepared to ride bikes to school. Often Priscilla would be sitting in the front yard watching the day begin. She'd sit in her lawn chair and watch the morning joggers, the various children walking and biking to school, the people hurrying to the bus stop to ride into the city for work. She'd sit and take it all in, watching the sunlight through the trees, enjoying the beginning of a new day. In the afternoon I'd see Priscilla sitting in her backyard, sometimes with her feet in a baby pool, watching the sunset and taking in the changing colors of the trees.

One day I walked over and sat next to Priscilla and asked her how she was getting along. "You know Mark, there's a part of me that is grateful for this cancer. It's slowed me down. It's caused me to sit and take in the world." Her eyes filled with tears, "It's so beautiful, Mark. It's just so beautiful...and I almost missed it. I almost missed how beautiful the world is."

Why is it that it is only when we get close to death that some of us are able to slow down and realize the miracle of this life? One of the gifts of prayer is that it slows our eyes to see, our ears to hear, and our hearts to feel. Prayer slows us so that gratitude can rise up and take hold of us. As we pray in thankfulness, we notice that gratitude is an attitude of the heart—it's a way of seeing, a way of being in the world.

You don't have to get cancer to know how precious the world is. You just need to be still for a moment and let prayer come over you. Soon you'll hear your own heart say, without effort, "Thank you."

SCRIPTURE

Verses to draw your spirit to God...

I trust in the steadfast love of God
forever and ever.
I will thank you forever,
because of what you have done.

PSALM 52:8-9

Open the gates of your heart with gratitude…

PSALM 100, ADAPTED BY NAN C. MERRILL

"Abba, I thank you for having heard me…"

JESUS, JOHN 11:41

PRAYER

Words to speak your heart to God…

Thanks

Listen

with the night falling we are saying thank you
we are stopping on the bridges to bow for the railings
we are running out of the glass rooms
with our mouths full of food to look at the sky
and say thank you
we are standing by the water looking out
in different directions.
back from a series of hospitals back from a mugging
after funerals we are saying thank you
after the news of the dead
whether or not we knew them we are saying thank you
looking up from tables we are saying thank you

in a culture up to its chin in shame
living in the stench it has chosen we are saying thank you
over telephones we are saying thank you
in doorways and in the backs of cars and in elevators
remembering wars and the police at the back door
and the beatings on stairs we are saying thank you
in the banks that use us we are saying thank you
with the crooks in office with the rich and fashionable
unchanged we go on saying thank you thank you
with the animals dying around us
our lost feelings we are saying thank you
with the forests falling faster than the minutes
of our lives we are saying thank you
with the words going out like cells of a brain
with the cities growing over us like the earth
we are saying thank you faster and faster
with nobody listening we are saying thank you
we are saying thank you and waving
dark though it is

W.S. MERWIN

MEDITATION

Reflections to open your mind to God...

As he was dying Abba Benjamin taught the disciples
his last lesson.
"Do this," he said, "and you will be saved:
Rejoice always,
pray constantly,
and in all circumstances
give thanks."

JOAN CHITTISTER

When my mother-in-law was a young woman, she
came to the point of not understanding why her family
was so interested in attending church. She could not
see the use in religion, and decided that she would no
longer believe in God. However, the day came when
she found herself sitting on the back steps looking up
into a magnificent fall sky and was overwhelmed by the
beauty that surrounded her. Suddenly she realized she
couldn't give up God because, "then there would be
no one to thank."

BARBARA CUMMINGS ST. JOHN

On the way to Jerusalem Jesus was going through the region between Samaria and Galilee. As he entered a village, ten lepers approached him. Keeping their distance, they called out, saying, "Jesus, Master, have mercy on us!" When he saw them, he said to them, "Go and show yourselves to the priests." And as they went, they were made clean. Then one of them, when he saw that he was healed, turned back, praising God with a loud voice. He prostrated himself at Jesus' feet and thanked him. And he was a Samaritan. Then Jesus asked, "Were not ten healed? But the other nine, where are they? Was none of them found to return and give praise to God except this foreigner?" Then he said to him, "Get up and go on your way; your faith has made you well."

LUKE 17:11-19

CONTEMPLATION

Exercises to help you spend time with God...

Saying Grace

God provides us with food that not only satisfies but delights. The Bible tells us God provided manna to the people of Israel. Jesus often used the image of a feast to communicate the life of God. Christians share bread and wine at Eucharist (the word Eucharist means "thanksgiving") as a way to remember and embody Jesus and his mission of love.

This is a prayer to help you embody gratitude. Go and get a piece of bread or fruit. Take a moment to reflect on how this food came into the world. If it is bread, reflect on the wheat that grew in the fields, the hands that milled the flour, and the people who delivered the bread to the market. If it is fruit, think of the sun and water that went into nourishing the fruit, and the farmers who cultivated and picked it. Take a moment to look at the food before you. Bring it to your nose and smell it. Think for a moment how God has created this food just for you. Now offer a prayer of thanks to God for what has been provided.

Now for a few moments savor this food. Eat it with a sense of God's delight and pleasure—no words are necessary. Allow a sense of deep gratitude to come over you as you enjoy what God has provided.

When you have finished eating, feel the fullness of your tummy and the taste of the food still present in your mouth. Then offer thanks to God for what has been given.

Next time you sit down at a meal, take a moment to allow this same awareness to come over you, then eat with a sense of gratefulness.

Noticing Gratitude

This prayer is a variation of the awareness examen from Chapter 7. In this prayer, you take the time to notice where moments of gratitude are breaking into your day.

Find a quiet place to pray. You may want to have a pen and journal. Take a few moments to relax and rest, gently becoming aware of God's presence, or the presence of Jesus, within and around you.

When you're ready, ask Jesus or the Holy Spirit to accompany you as you go over the previous day—from when you first woke up, to this moment right now. As you go through the day in prayer allow this question to arise, "For what moment was I most grateful?" Allow little things to emerge: A smile from a stranger, the sunlight through a window, a kind act from someone in your family, an engaging conversation. Choose one of these moments to meditate on. What does it have to teach you about your life with God? Don't force anything—just be open and let the moment arise that seems to hold the most gratitude. You may want to journal your reflections. Now offer thanks to God for each of these moments.

Notice what you are like at the end of this prayer. What is it like to take in these gratitudes from the day? At the end of this prayer ask this question, "God, what is your invitation to me?

Giving Thanks

This prayer invites you to reflect on all you are thankful for. Take out a journal and a pen or pencil, and reflect on the following question: "What am I grateful for?" Now write down everything that comes to you, whether it be big or small. As you write, be as specific as possible. For example, my list might be: My wife, Jill, my daughter's hugs, the smell of a wood fire, good coffee, the town where we live, my ability to write, my health, hearing my son play piano, my friend Frank, the flowers blooming in the backyard, the church I grew up in, etc. List as many things as come to you.

When you've finished writing, prepare yourself for a time of prayer. After a few moments of quiet, become aware of God's presence. Then, as you're ready, take out your list. As you look at each item, say the following sentence either aloud or within you, "Thank you, God, for [the first item on your list]." Pause and allow gratitude to come over you for this blessing in your life. Then, when you're ready, go to the second item on your list and pray, "Thank you, God, for _____." Pray each of these items with heartfelt care. Allow yourself to fill with gratitude for all that has been given to you.

When you finish your list, simply close your eyes and bask in gratitude. Let this spirit of thankfulness be your prayer. No further words are necessary. Then, as your prayer time comes to a close, let this question rise up within you: "God, what is your invitation to me?" See if there is some way (some action, a new attitude, etc.) God is inviting you to respond to this prayer.

Sources

W.S. Merwin, *The Rain in the Trees* (Albert A. Knopf, 1998).

Joan Chittister, *Illuminated Life* (Orbis, 2000).

Barbara Cummings St. John, cited in Catherine Whitmire, *Plain Living* (Sorin, 2001).

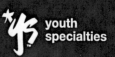

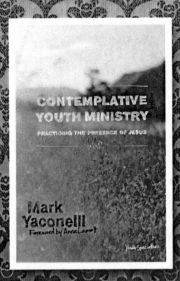

Youth pastors are growing tired of simply providing a ministry to distract and entertain teenagers. There is a growing desire for deeper, more authentic forms of adolescent discipleship. Grounded in experience with real churches, this book chronicles the journey of more than a dozen youth ministries working to move Christian spirituality out of the retreat center and into the youth room.

Growing Souls
Experiments in Contemplative Youth Ministry

Mark Yaconelli
978-0-310-27328-8

Visit www.youthspecialties.com
or your local bookstore.

youth
specialties

CPSIA information can be obtained
at www.ICGtesting.com
Printed in the USA
LVOW07s1118271017
553926LV00010B/151/P